DADDY'S LITTLE GIRL

A True Love Story About
Crissa A. Jackson

J A M E S   J A C K S O N

ISBN 978-1-6678-5739-8 (paperback)
ISBN 978-1-0980-8254-3 (digital)

Christian Faith Publishing
832 Park Avenue
Meadville, PA 16335
www.christianfaithpublishing.com

Printed in the United States of America

PREFACE

Thank you for opening this book, which is all about a true love story. The author hopes this book helps you to find true love in your personal life. He is so happy that you are beginning to desire to read this book about love. There is something that you need to know right up front about the truth in this book.

The truth is, God is the author of this book and daddy is the messenger who is writing everything down that the Holy Spirit has given him concerning this true love story about Daddy's Little Girl. Most people think that love is so cold these days, but in this true love story, you will find that love has heated up to the point where daddy's little girl catches on fire.

He is a writing Evangelist under the covering of Liberty Evangelistic Ministries which this book is an extension of the ministry. This book also serves the ministry by reaching the moms, dads, sons and daughters all over the world.

The money that each book makes, will be deposited into the ministry account (Liberty Evangelistic Ministries) to be used to promote the ministry. This book will help those who have special needs and promote God's Kingdom by showing love as the Holy Spirit leads the ministry.

ACKNOWLEDGEMENTS

I would like to thank God for my granddaughter Crissa, who has grown up to be a loving caring person to God's people. She is full of ambition, striving very hard with the help of her father in her young life to reach her goal. With God's help she is receiving all she has work hard for and I give you this word, keep your hands in God's hand and you will be blessed always.

Marilyn Jackson
Grandmother

"Beast mode - I love you girl!"

Mar

Crissa, you are my precious gift from God and I am so thankful for you. I love that you are my daughter. I am so very proud of you. Forever loving you!

Mom

Crissa is doing what she has always loved since before she could even walk - playing with a basketball. She has gone from the playground, to school gymnasiums, to arenas all across the country. But she didn't stop there. She has now taken her love of basketball, and seemingly magical manipulation and control of the basketball itself, and transformed it into an international platform where she influences the masses on a daily basis with her message of love, positivity, and acceptance while seamlessly providing entertainment to both

young and old people around the world. She is a proven role model for anyone in any shape or form. Her story is a true testament that dreams do come true. And though she is my younger sister, she is still my hero and serves as a day-to-day inspiration and reminder of what can be accomplished through hard work, dedication, and perseverance. Love you, Crissa. You make me proud to call you family.

Jay

DADDY! Thanks so much for being the best dad ever, for always being there for me, for being the best teacher, and for all the love you show me! Congrats on the book!

I LOVE YOU!
YOUR BABY GIRL
Crissa Jackson

INTRODUCTION

THE PURPOSE BEHIND THE BOOK

D addy hopes you are ready to be swept off your feet with one of the most exciting books of the century, it is about love power with transparency for your eyes and heart only, so you can understand and know "Love" in the twenty-first century.

This is the year 2020, where it is known for its sight beyond sight, but this book will be published in 2022. This is the year of perfect vision and foresight base on how you are able to see "Love" when you read this book that sincerely talks about love at first sight.

First of all, daddy would like to thank you for taking out the time to read this book, it is about his daughter, "Crissa Jackson and her" true love story of how she became a star over time because of love. As she continues this day to shine like she has never shined before in her life through social media, he wants you to know very early, that he was bless to be the love writer, the messenger of love for this book.

You might as well know the truth up front about daddy's little girl, according to their experience and try to understand what happen when she was six years old. This book is supposed to give you inspiration of love from God the Holy Spirit because everything that was written in this book gives God the glory and the praise.

The whole truth and nothing but the truth is that it was God that gave daddy and his little girl the inspiration and love that provided them all that they needed to make the love journey one day at a time. Daddy looks back twenty five years and can still see his little girl in his mind, full of excitement with love, asking him the big question.

"Daddy, you trained Jay, can you train me?" She created one of the most beautiful pictures of her face and body language, this he had not seen in a very long time from anyone. It was like God helping him to capture that love moment that he needed to see and feel in his heart.

He really believes this book is going to light up your family life with a true love story about a little girl who believes in her dreams and vision and a daddy who believes in his little girl. The book is a winning combination of daddy and his little girl binding together with love cords that can't be broken.

This is just a part of my introduction to you. What that's really supposed to mean to you as you read, you will see and understand how the power of love builds relationships. This book will help you to focus on the love between a little girl and her daddy.

They both had dreams and visions about how together they can reach their goals and succeed in a particular sport. The book will enable you to apply the information that you read to your little girl or boy.

The book is a true love story about daddy and his little girl and not a fairy tale about something that is fake, phony, or just made up. This book has a love story that will open up your heart and mind to the commitment and dedication of sports.

This love story will enable you to tap into how you can take it one day, week and month at a time, acting out true love until it becomes one year at a time. This book will help you to be consistent in falling in love over and over again with each other and the sport.

The best thing in life that could happen to daddy and his little girl was being connected with the hope and vision of love cords that can not be broken for the rest of their lives. This book will help you develop love cords that will cause you to be successful.

Daddy and his little girl knew as long as it will take them to succeed, they both were willing to pay the piper to be able to dance to the love music that they made together to produce good basketball. They both did the love dance to the training exercise, keeping with the beat of the heart to the love drums. It empowered them figuratively speaking, to be able to love to work together while training and practicing.

In other words, they were more than willing to work hard together, believing in each other to do their part as they looked into each other eyes and into each other hearts every day, it enabled them to tap into the spiritual senses of love.

In the beginning, daddy and his little girl had to trust in the five natural and spiritual senses (touch, taste, smell, hear and sight to start out the relationship, and they knew in their heart that they should not despise new beginnings.

As they started to practice and train every day in the very beginning, he started to notice that they needed a routine with the ball. God gave them the insight and ability how to train with the ball at the track.

When they touched the basketball, it was as though God gave dad what drills to do and gave his little girl a feel for handling the ball on the track and shooting the ball at the basketball court. He believes that love and prayer for training and practicing kicked in early and gave them a blessing in disguise.

It was almost as if God deposited the gift into the both of them at the same time. At this point of time, they were able to hear and taste the words of basketball, they were able to discern the words by the love that they have for the game of basketball.

Whatever God did when he deposited the gifts or awakened the gift, he connected the both of them. Daddy liked to think that God connected their gift with their love that they had for the game. Daddy liked to think of the game of basketball as a special love place in the heart and the mind of him and his little girl.

Daddy knew that there was a personal empowerment that came on them when they act in the love of the game. In other words, communicating with each other with love, help them to understand what they should do on the track and on the court.

They always talked about the difference ways to dribble one or two balls around the track. His daughter trusted him while both trusted the Holy Spirit for everything by faith through love. He was so proud of her for her hunger and thirst to love and learn how to play the game called basketball.

Both of them could feel the power of love working from their senses of touch and taste that they had acquire for training and practicing in order to be successful. Remember, both of them started out not knowing what to do and where to go.

Her dad did not have the money to go to camps or places that would charge for training. They both had to train outside at the track, hills, stairs, and the outside courts. The both of them went looking for any place outside that they could start training.

The both of them did not care about what the place look like, they just wanted some place that they could call their training court or track. They were very happy and proud when they found a track and a court outdoors.

When they found the outdoors, the both of them did not know anything about training, the dad knew about basic training in boot camp from the military, fundamental training in ministry and common sense.

In other words, both of them were able to have their own experience from their love senses, so that they would be able to draw closer to training and practicing with the ball. The background and backbone of this story when all the dust clears the air is the foundation of love that enabled both of them to be drawn and driven by the greatest power on the face of this earth.

In this book, daddy will always be expressing love in everything he talks about in the true love story of daddy and his little girl. Because of love, daddy and his little girl could also sense the spirit of hope, opportunity and success.

Every time they would come together to train on the track and workout on the basketball court, they were becoming like two magnets drawn together, making it harder to be separated. They became dedicated and committed to each other, which deepened their love for each another.

Every day, every week, every month, and every year they would become closer and closer to each other. This book will also reveal how daddy and his little girl received the secret ingredient about God's love that gave them tremendous motivation, spiritual energy, unbelievable strength, and powerful endurance through training and practicing.

Speaking of happiness, this book is full of happy times because the journey that daddy and his little girl chosen had many adventures and excitements that brought tears of joy and happiness. Success and victories were happening all the time for daddy and his little girl because of the commitment, dedication, loyalty, faithfulness, and consistency of loving each other during the hard times.

This is a very happy book, so happy, he almost thought of it as a fairy tale story about a little girl who dreamed that one day she would become a star basketball player, having no signs or evidence to show that she was star material.

She was short in stature, very thin and light in weight and her father knew nothing about basketball, having no special contacts or connection to get help and no money to pay anyone to help her or him. The most important fact is that she was only six years old when she asked her daddy the big question.

"Could you teach me, daddy, to play basketball?" Instead of him crying from the bottom of his soul, he first looked and then he just starred at her for a few seconds, he did not believe that he just heard her ask him to train her in the game of basketball.

So, this is one of the reasons why he wanted to start writing this book as a fairy tale story about a little girl who believed and asked the question, "could you teach me, daddy, to play basketball?" By the words from her heart, she gave birth from a fairy tale to a true love story.

It was also the power of her tongue that enable her to give birth to a true love story. He believed that she could do anything but fail if she could get her daddy to help her to love like he never loved before. From her sincere question, was created a true love story about her love life.

Daddy knew that all daddies are not going to get this, but today he still cries out from his heart, the tears he shares still fill his eyes as he remembers to tell the true love story of daddy and his little girl. This is a true love story that will change the way everyone approaches the love of the game.

All he knows is that once upon time, a fairy tale story was only a thought, ideal, or maybe just her wild imagination, but never the less, it turned out to be one of the best true love stories that ever been written and it is still the real deal in the twenty-first century.

Daddy was given one open window and door by God, because his little girl acted by faith to chase the dream and vision, believed that God's love believes all things, hope all things, endure all things, and the best of all, she learn that the love of the game will never failed daddy and his little girl.

Note: Insert "The Message" right after the Introduction.

THE AUTHOR MESSAGE

The author knew when he started writing this book, it was perfect timing for him to help you who is reading to know and understand, this is a real-life true love story about a daddy and his little girl. He really thought it would be very important to you if he would take a few lines and chapters to write about a true love story. Just remember, the little girl is all grown up on social media.

He wanted you to always know in the back of your mind that this book is about the love of daddy and his little girl, and he wanted that love to reach out to every daddy and mommy. As you continue to read, he wants you to know that he thinking how you are going to be blessed by what you read.

He will try with all of his heart to connect you to the only power and authority that believes all things, hopes all things, endures all things, and will never fail any mommy or daddy, boy or girl. It is very important, especially when you have knowledge and understand love's mission from God to you.

God's purpose of designing love was not only to draw all people unto him, but give all people the opportunity to let love help you to be the greatest in any sport of your choice. He wants to implement his love as a tool for your success in sports.

The book was written to all the daddies and mommies out there who has a little girl or little boy and don't know what to do when their child is inspired and encouraged to play sports. Does your little girl or boy want to be prepared to be the very best in the sport of their choice?

The book is written to all those moms or dads that don't know what to do or how to make the right choice. When a mom or dad doesn't have the skills to train or coach their child personally, it is time for this book to inspire you to love to the point where you will trust God for your son or daughter.

It was also written for all the little girls or boys who also do not know what it takes, if they have a burning heart's desire to play the sport of their choice. This book will introduce you and your kids to the power of love.

The principles that are in this book, you will be able to apply today, once you see yourself wanting to train and practice at the track and on the court, it will help you to choose a place of your choice. The spirit of love according to this book, will show you how your five natural and spiritual senses will help you.

Imagine yourself outdoor at the track and surrounded by hills, trying to reach the goals and complete the tasks from your heart. You will be able to touch, taste, see, smell, and hear from your mind and heart, a sense of how the ball is working for you. It almost sounds magical, but that is what true love will do for you.

You're not only running around the track, but you are dribbling up and down hills doing distance, building speed, and building the legs to carry you up and down the court. That is what loves energy does for those who learn to love the sport from their heart.

The book will soon begin to reveal to you how God will help you to begin to be able to see, hear, taste, touch, and smell with both the natural senses and spiritual senses of love in the beginning of your new journey. The book will help you to connect the spiritual dots of love and basketball training and practice, for any sport you choose.

You can become great, if you learn to apply the love of God with common sense. The book will share with you, that anything you do, you got to have faith working through love and that love will work through your five spiritual senses one day at a time.

The author hopes and believes that this book will open up your heart, mind, and build the strength within your soulish realm. This is a message to all the daddies and little girls in the whole wide world, this book is a game changer, and he hopes this book would set your entire sports world with a "love fire, that burns baby burn."

This love fire will give you the ability to quench all of your spiritual hunger and thirst, it will drive you closer to seek after the power of the love of God in sports. According to this book, it is only God's love that can produce success in sports and raise up the standard and bar for your success.

You will never experience anything like this before in all of your days. When you read this material, ask God to reveal to you about the true love of God that is buried in this book like buried treasure. This could be your spiritual map to a love treasure.

The author prayed that all the daddies and the little girls would discover the truth and nothing but the truth so help them God, it is all about the buried treasure of God's love in this book. When you seek God for help, he will reveal to you that all the daddies and little girls are on their way to a very exciting adventure after reading this book.

Your love journey of sport, will be revelation of your love, because of God's true love that is buried very deep throughout the pages in this book for you to discover. This love that he's sharing is facts, that you need to know concerning the truth about love.

True love power will allow you to discover how many others before you manage to become very successful in sports. This concept and principles of love, is the only way for you to be able to get the job done right when it comes to the sports world.

Daddy always felt that if you love something strong enough, bad enough, then nothing will stop the drive that you will have inside of you to become successful. Daddy believes that love is the spiritual magnet and force that will draw you to do whatever it takes or whatever needs to be done for success.

True love, will have you take the second mile and the third or whatever it takes. Once God deposits his love in every daddy and his little girl, it will cause you to have the greatest love relationship of all times in any sport of your choice.

You will be able to do things together that you have never imagined. You will be able to go places together that you have never dreamed of while you were sleeping. You will be able to build something special together that will never change in a life time.

Your bonds and cords shall never be broken on this earthly journey. You will be able to connect spiritually throughout all eternity or as long as you are on this earth together. The both of you will be able to go places together you never been yet, see people you both never saw yet, talk about things you never talk about yet, because that is what true love does.

The book will become a learning tool to help your little boy and girl who dreams and have visions to be successful in sports. This is a true love story that will capture your heart, mind, and soul because it will point and direct you to the greatest love moments and movements of all time in the game of sports.

This love story will give your imagination enough food if you are hungry, and water if you are really thirsty, to strengthen your love relationships with sports and family. This book will reveal to you how daddies and his little girls will be able to survive, not having any skills.

This is one of those love stories of sacrifice and hard work that takes one day at a time until you turn it into one week at a time, sharing true love to each other. The book is going to take all of your imagination and give it some positive love substance.

This love substance is going to energize the bunny rabbit that is inside of your imagination, who likes to go hopping around with joy

unspeakable and full of happiness. Can you truly imagine how this true love can produce joy of happiness in the sport of your choice?

Speaking of happiness, this book is full of happy times, the love journey that you are going to embark on will have so many adventures and excitements that will bring tears of joy and happiness. Success and victories will happen for you all the time because of the commitment, dedication, loyalty, faithfulness, and consistency of you falling in love over and over again with the sport of your choice.

SECTION ONE

CRISSA THE LITTLE BABY
PART 1
A TRUE LOVE STORY

CHAPTER ONE

A STAR IS BORN

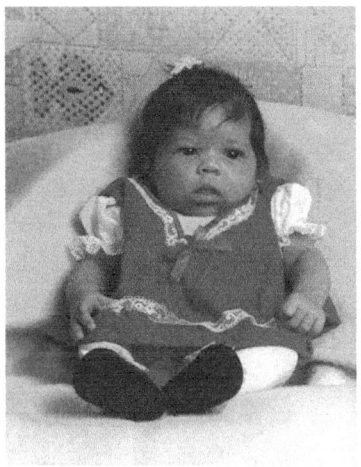

O nce upon a time, in a faraway place, in the land east of the County of San Diego, California, there was to be born a "**Love Star.**" It was a place not known to many people, but it was known by God that one day, there would be born a baby girl on October 26, 1989, who was one of the prettiest babies of that day.

Did you know that God calls each baby a gift? It is stated that the gift will bring you joy, peace, love and harmony, it was design by God to give every parent the love that they need to build and establish relationships with their child.

This gift was born with straight black hair, beautiful bronze skin with big lovely eyes, and she was a sight to lay eyes on. This baby was a love gift to her mommy and daddy, a gift that would strive on God's love to fulfill her fantasy and dream to become a love star.

By faith through love, it was predestined for this baby to be born at this time, because of the many prayers, fasting, and giving birth to a new ministry called "New Born Christian Fellowship' was a good sign to the Jackson family regarding her birth.

The wife found out that she was pregnant with her fourth child, it was the ninth month, she would be ready to give birth to a love star and not know it. When the Jackson's started the new ministry, it was a season where God was giving birth to a child and a church.

This was also their love season of sowing and planting love seeds into the heart of the people in the East County of San Diego through the ministry. This is a true love story about a little baby girl who was born as the fourth child with two other sisters (Aleena and Marilyn) and a brother (Jay).

This true love story, connects God's love to their hearts and feelings, to learn to love sports and dream to be successful one day. Now there were a lot of seeds planted and sown into the new baby girl before and after birth.

She was even nurture by way of reading, praying, fasting, singing, praising, and worshipping by her mother and the father during her nine months while she was still in her stomach. He truly believes that his little girl was being prepared, shaped, molded, and gifted for her destiny by God.

His new born baby girl was a gift to the family, a little baby girl who was given the name Crissa which means a follower of Christ, look it up. This true love story is all about how God deposited his love and gift inside her to become a star.

It all started during her first year when she was able to learn how to walk, talk, and grew to be a very funny and fun baby. She would always demonstrate her love character during the process of her growth by making things fun.

During her second year, she was learning to potty train and you could see the love that she had for her family by always showing off, she was able to go to the bathroom on her own, and that meant a lot to us, no one had to change her diaper anymore.

The third year, she was able to talk in short sentences, expressing her love to her family and holding conversations with everyone. During her fourth year, she was now communicating with everyone that was in the family and becoming her own person with love that brought joy and happiness to her family.

She nursed to she was four years old, and she wanted to be held all the time, she always wanted to be loved, and they gave her their very best during her first five years. Now all of her siblings were taught and trained by this principle, "the first five years of the child's heart must be developed in love."

In her fifth year, the family could see her love development in her personality and character by the way she talked and acted towards everyone in the family. Her first five years were built on love; as a matter of fact, her parents' goals were to enforce love to her through every area of her life.

Mom and dad knew that love would establish the foundation in her heart and that same love would establish her dreams, hopes, goals, and visions for the rest of her life time. They knew that the time has come for her to be released to go to school.

This was her chance to shine and nothing could hold her back because she was taught and trained in God's love family to be successful. During the 1990's, the school system was set up that if your child turned five years of age before December of that year, you could start school at four years old.

She started school in September at the age of four because her next birthday was October 26, 1994, please do the math! There was a negative thought that would always be stated, when a child starts school early, less than five years old, they usually are the ones that have complications.

But the family knew that wasn't the case for her, she was trained to love in the family. There is a concept and theory about how love shapes the character and personality, giving the person all the virtues, knowledge, and understanding how loves works in the mind, heart, and the character.

In other words, her faith taught her that after a person is born of water through their mother's womb, that person still must be born of the spirit of God's love. She was taught to follow the teaching of her lord and savior according to Romans 10:9-10 to believe, confess and accept Jesus as savior.

Then she had to be taught according to 2 Corinthians 5:17, her old nature became a new nature, and that new nature is the love of God. Her new love nature will develop her love character and personality for the rest of her life.

The author, believes that love is located in the heart of the soulish realm in her body, and that new love nature was prepared to help her to overcome any challenge that she was going to face in the world of basketball. Please try to understand that love helps a person to have the right passion, feelings, and the sensitivity for every area of the sport.

He remembers taking her to her first day at school, she was a little shy, but she was ready for school. She had two older sisters and one older brother, they would help her to practice her math, reading and writing, preparing her to meet the challenge in school.

She could count her numbers and sing, read her alphabets, which made her ready to go to school to make her family proud, her family wanted her to experience the best adventure at school that has ever been known to any child. Note, who could have asked for a child who had the heart and spirit of an adventurer?

During her first year at school, she was the happiest baby girl any parent could ask for, you could see how love was working in her and through her relationships with the students, teachers, and staff at her school.

She was always bringing home good reports about here grades and character, and every time they had parent's night, she was always excited about her projects that were on the school board and display. Her teacher would always talk about her personality and energy.

This was a very good sign for mom and dad, she was the love baby and was learning from her family to be the best love child that she could be in the classroom and out of the classroom. Trying to please her was not hard during her growth.

She went to three birthdays every year since she was born, plus her own birthday. She had two sisters and one brother to play with every day. She would have fun telling on her brother and her sisters when they do something wrong to anyone.

She was always focusing on keeping the rules of operation in her home every day of the week. If anybody (he is talking about the parents and the siblings) would do anything that she thought was wrong and not fair, she would notify somebody what they did or tell a parent that something was wrong.

Her word was like the bible and she would tell the truth and nothing but the truth so helps her God. She was operating in love that cares which was taught to her at a very early age as a baby growing up to be an amazing love child.

So far, everything was looking good for her and she was very active during children's church, and when she was three years old, she received Jesus Christ as her savior. Later that year, she received the Baptism of the Holy Spirit.

During elementary school and children's church, she was having a normal happy child love life. Love started to give her the dedication, commitment; loyalty, faithfulness, and self-control that she needed to make all the right decision, she was growing each day as a promise child to follow her dreams and visions.

Love did not make her growth come instantly, it help her to grow as a fruit grows when it is pruned daily, weekly, or monthly. True love has helped her to become constraint in every area that will cause her difficulty. Love has become her secret weapon by all means, it was developing her heart.

She discovers that love is the most powerful force on planet earth, because love is God. This kind of love will transform her from liking to loving, she just has to follow her dreams, visions and let love be her guide.

You can just introduce yourself to God's love by talking to God, asking him for love to show your future destiny. This kind of love story will help you to understand why love is so important in a child's life, especially when it comes to vision and dreams.

Another thing that is important is the first five years of your child life, you must develop love, it will give the child a strong love foundation, they are going to need it when they leave the home to start school or sports.

When it comes to sports, especially when you realize what you want to play, it is the first five years of practicing and training in love, you must build your foundation for the love of the sport. The point is, when you are a baby you need to learn to do the things babies does when it comes to growing as a love child.

This book is going to give you knowledge and help you understand that you must learn to love and be able to build on that love foundation for the sport of your choice for the rest of your life. One of the keys to the love of God, you got to plant and sow love into your heart and nurture it until there are signs of growth and maturity.

Now, he wants to inform you early in the first chapter, he knows that any person can become a target for the devil to attack, the devil does not want anyone to grow up displaying the love of God. So, God warns you now to start protecting your heart with love from anything negative aiming at your life.

This is a fact, the seed of love was deposited into her heart as a baby, so she can grow to spread those seeds of love all over the world and follow her dream and vision as God gifted her with basketball to be a "**Love Star**."

CHAPTER TWO

THE GIFT FROM GOD

T his part of the story is about the gift of God, his gift who was born into a family that dedicate all the babies to the love of God in Jesus. This love gift began to change the way she was going to become successful.

The Jackson family declared, decree, and proclaim that their home and everyone that lived in their home would serve the lord Jesus Christ, this is true in everything that they do, and when the gift leaves the home, the gift would have a love platform and love foundation to choose their own love journey.

The Jackson family worked hard together to made sure that a lot of love and prayers were offer up to God for the gift that was in her mother's belly, just like it was done for the rest of her siblings. The children didn't have much choice in the matter.

He always thanked God for the prayers of his Christian friends, the natural family and the spiritual church family. From the beginning of the conception of the gift, the gift was nurtured in love, prayer, fasting, praise and worship.

Mom and dad always focused on a lot of worship and praise during those nine months that was aimed towards the gift for specific reasons. One reason, so the blessing of the Lord would be released upon her life.

The family according to Matthew 19:14 and Mark 10:15 wanted to make her first and more important, making sure spiritually that there would be no complication during the nine months or at delivery in the name of Jesus.

Her mother was a prayer warrior and a worship leader at that time, during the pregnancy at home and at the church. They say, the baby is alive early at some point during the pregnancy and is able to receive from the parent things that can encourage their growth physically and spiritually during that pregnancy.

It is said that pregnancy can be a learning curve for the gift before she is born and that was exactly what they had in mind for her spiritually. Their God-given purpose for the gift was to minister and love the gift through the spirit of God, way before the gift arrived, and that is exactly what they done.

This is a fact and a principle that the church has an ordinance establish and they call it baby dedication service. This service is done for all new born gifts; the purpose is to give back the gift to God so the blessing would be on that child.

Her parents would do no different than what they did for the other siblings. They were more experienced and mature as they witnessed positive results that happened to the older siblings as gifts, when they sought early spiritual preparation.

The gift arrived (born) on October 26, 1989 at the Grossmont Hospital in La Mesa, California, the east county of San Diego; they knew she was very special, they poured a lot of love into her during the whole nine months.

They even took the gift home to begin to nurse with praise and worship tapes, they continued to pour into her spirit love to help her grow spiritually. Training has now been put into spiritual motion according to Proverbs 2:6 for the Jackson family.

In their home, they have planned to get her familiar with the former years of experience from training her older siblings as gifts, in order to build a love foundation. It was her time to get a strong foundation of God's love and mercy according to Matthew 7:24 in her heart.

As they normally would do, they took her every Sunday to the church's nursery ministry where they read, sung, and worshipped God in her presence according to Acts 2:42. When she turned two years old, her learning curve was growing in the lord.

As soon after she turned three years old, she accepted the lord as her savior because she understood the gospel message of Jesus dying for her sins and in order for her to be saved; she had to accept him as her savior according to Romans 10:9, 10.

Not only did she accept him, but later that year, she was baptized in the Holy Spirit and spoke in tongues according to Acts 1:8. She had her older siblings helping her to get it done, they all were on the same page.

When her siblings told him, he just laughed, they said they told her what to say and how to say it and she did it. So, right in front of him they share how their baby sister spoke by repeating whatever they said out of their mouth. He just fell out laughing!

It was always beautiful to hear from her teacher and her siblings, she did all those things in the name of Jesus. For the next few years, they were getting all kinds of praise reports of her successes in her class rooms, both Sunday school and later Elementary School.

Now the Jackson's invested in the Christian cartoon collection called "McGee and Me" ministry tapes that were on the market for that day. These tapes covered all the bible stories and they were in cartoon character and the kids love it.

Jesus said, "Suffer your daughter/son to come unto me and forbid her/him not, for such is the kingdom of God." Another passage states that except she/he becomes a little child of God, she/he cannot enter into the kingdom of God.

Another passage, which is more familiar is, "trained up your daughter/son in the way she/he should go, and when she/he matures spiritually, they will not depart from their training." The Jackson's knew that they had their work cut out for them.

They also knew, it would be a lot of joy, peace, hope and faith and the love of God would draw them to the place where they would make sure that she was getting all the love that they could mustard up during her growing pains.

They knew, she needed God's love especially during the first five years, which will deepen her foundation with roots of love way deep down in her heart, which would give her the ability to build on for the rest of her life.

Crissa first five years were the most important time of her childhood and during those years they knew that Crissa would be open to learn especially from the scriptures and from her mother and dad's spiritual life style.

They practiced having everyone in the house to represent Christian education and living the Christian life as best as they could. Dad knew, it would have a positive impact on her life spiritually and it would give her love knowledge, love understanding, and love wisdom.

This kind of teaching and training was necessary to get through the most difficult times in her childhood as she got older, according to Matthew 22:37. It was just a matter of time that she would see the wonderful benefits of love.

At the age of six, you could see her love shaping and sharpening her character, she asked daddy to teach and train her for basketball as a career at the age of six. Her love had grown inside of her during her first five years, according to 1 Peter 2:2.

Dad knew, looking back at that time and moment that she was acting out her prayers and faith in God that accumulated over the years, showing her parents that she was ready to make her move in life (Luke 398 12:48).

That was a powerful time and movement for Crissa, she believed in God to help her with the love she had for basketball. Remember that Jesus said, that you can do all things through him because it is Jesus who gives you the love that you need to be able to have the strength mentally, physically, and spiritually.

At this point in her life, you need to understand how the Spirit of God was supplying all of her basketball needs. She also felt that much known is much required, and she acted on the love gift that God had put in her to discover and developed her game of basketball.

The bible says, many that are led by the spirit of God are the children of God. At the age of six, she probably did not know what she was feeling at that time, but one thing was sure, love was leading her to play the game called basketball. Love has connected her or drawn her to the place in her heart to ask daddy the question.

The more he thought about that, the more he could see spiritually to discern that it was the love of God that could make a divine intervention happen like that in her heart. The following year at the age of seven, she changed her name to star, which was another act of faith through love.

During the following years she made her email address star. For years, she took on the character of a young female basketball star everywhere she went in the San Diego County and the people treated her like a star.

The bible says, there is love power in the tongue, in other words, by the words she spoke, she created her own image of who she is going to be, and she even spoke it into existence having a positive image in her God-given imagination.

He didn't know whether or not that she understood the power of the tongue according to the scripture in her younger years, but he does know that she has the faith through love to believe in her future destiny.

He just wanted to add that she wanted to speak faith into existence and she call that which is not as though it is and did not doubt in Jesus name. The bible says, as a girl thinks, so is she. You will become what you say out of your mouth, especially if you say it all the time in faith.

She would always talk about how great of a basketball player she wanted to be and by her own mouth, she called that which was not as though it was hers for the taking. By doing that, over time, she created her own image of a female star basketball player in her sport.

He knew that if she could see it, believe it, then she would be able to achieve it through the love of God by hard work. Now he would like to remind you that this takes faith that works through the love of God only.

He states, the love of God will give a person the opportunity to be able to dedicate, commit, loyal and faithful to the love of the game only. All he could think about every time that he was with Crissa, she wants to be a basketball star.

She began her career with prayer during her early years because when she started training at six years old, there was no little girl basketball team at any school in all of the county of San Diego. They search everywhere and could not find one school.

They were on their own and all they could do was pray, God had someone come to the track during her training at the age of seven and told them that the Grossmont School was having a girls' little league basketball summer camp teams.

He said, "Wow," and looked at her, and she began to thank God in her own way for that opportunity that came out of no-were. He began to notice her connection with God by her reaction and response when she wanted something to happen in her life concerning basketball.

Her mother and father were always praying, especially when they started their own ministry called New Born Christian Fellowship. They knew that the ministry was going to bless her in her search for success in the game of basketball.

After the age of seven, daddy became her only pastor and teacher, and there was no one else teaching her but her mother, sisters and children's church. Her brother was always using sarcasm with her, trying to make her laugh.

She loved it most of the time, but her brother would always encourage her when it came to basketball. She was always trying to be a bible teacher or finance officer like her siblings. Her sisters and brother would not allow her to take their spiritual duty on Sunday.

So, she sat on the side lines in the chair watching them and saying to them, "you can't stop me from playing basketball." She would always lead prayer in the family every time she would get the opportunity and that was far between.

She just wanted to show her siblings that she too could pray like them at a very young age. The bible says, each generation is weaker but yet wiser, and he could see that she was tapping into the wisdom when it came to church and basketball.

Somehow, she was very focused and determined from the very start. She was always looking for her break through from God in every area of life and basketball. She was a fire ball that was always ready to serve the lord out of love, commitment, and dedication to basketball.

She also started out being very shy, she was the youngest, but over time she grew, but not completely out of her shyness. She was very prudent, especially around people that she didn't know and that was expected from her.

She never missed children's church because it was her way of life. The bible says, if you give of yourself to him, he would cause people to bless you thirty, sixty and a hundred folds. She knew of nothing else but to go to church every Sunday, because that's what her family did all of her known life.

They knew that it was just a matter of time for her to see the manifestation of her blessing for the commitment that she has given unto the lord through church and basketball. She was always happy because the godly life she established put her in a love environment where she could feel the presence of God.

God was helping her character and personality to grow for something special and when she was six years old it came to fruition that the thing God had for her was love for basketball. She was spiritually institutionalized; she did the same thing spiritually every Wednesday and Sunday of the week.

Even though she was shy, she was still trained in prayer, fasting, and reading the scriptures. She knew how to seek God face at an early aged, the plan dad got from God for her would help her to build a personal relationship with him concerning the love of basketball.

As time went by, they decided to move from California to Pennsylvania, which had girls' basketball in elementary schools and again that was another prayer answer for her because California did not have girls' basketball in elementary schools.

Because he was praying and fasting during this time in his life, it enabled him to see the hand of God move for her over time. When she got to Pennsylvania, she added fasting and more prayer to her life, and nothing got in her way to stop her from playing basketball.

The very next miracle that happened in her life, was the opportunity for her for the first time to leave the United States with the organization called People to People Student Ambassador Program. She flew to Amsterdam to play basketball and returned with the MVP Trophy and you could see that she had stars in her eyes and coming out of her heart.

She would tell her dad year after year how she is praying for strength, courage, and opportunity to be able to get through the training and practice with her daddy. Especially during her first five years of training and practicing as God was helping her to endure.

Most of her practices were spent by herself and she trained alone with the Holy Spirit. She would always tell him how blessed she was to learn from the Holy Spirit. Crissa and daddy would always pray before and after practices and training until she began to do it on her own.

She realizes and understood that her father, who she asked to train her, was not a basketball trainer, but he was a man of God. He told her that he had to go to God and he would give him what to do and how to get it done.

She was very young and she also, as time went on started trusting God for her training and development. He remembers one time, he told her that he carried his bible with him wherever he went so that he could always be reading the word of God and that was part of his training and discipline.

So, he told her that the Spirit of God told him to tell her "to carry the basketball with you wherever you go and your hands and the ball will become one." He knew, she had a sense of how the Holy Spirit was going to lead him with her.

She carried that ball to school, church, and friends' homes; she never let that ball out of her sight. She brought a gym bag so whenever she was not dribbling the ball or was tired of carrying the ball, she would carry it in a gym bag.

She did not only believe him, she accepted the fact that she was being train by God the Holy Spirit through her daddy, and that was all right with her. Her love for the game was the same love she had for God, because the bible said, God is love.

Jesus said; love the lord your God with all of your heart, mind, strength, and soul, based on that teaching, she was able to love, and that love enabled her to be drawn to basketball. And that love through her basketball training and practicing was acted out in everything she did on and off the track and court.

He was able to see her with his own eyes, developing just like the scripture said when it stated, when she was a child, she acted like a child, she understood like a child, but when she began to practice and train in the love words of God, on the track and court, she began to put away childish things and began to grow and mature in the game and skill of basketball.

In other words, Crissa game was coming into fruition (a point in which a plan or project is realized), a time in her life where she was now seeing results from all of the hard work and sacrifice, she did spiritually, mentally, and physically.

All you have to do is remember that all the hard work and sacrifice Crissa was doing is all about the love of God that was in her. If you can comprehend this, then you are right on point and well on your way to a successful career in your child's life of sports.

The scripture said, love believes all things, and she believed everything that he was telling her, not only because he was her daddy, but because she could see, feel, and discern the kind of love training that her daddy would ask her to do so she could develop her basketball skills.

He knew, she needed to do specific drills during training on the track and the court, and it was revealed to him by the Holy Spirit what he should do to bring increase in her training and practicing. There was one thing that she needed to be, and that was the best she could be in order to be a star.

She carried that hope to the track and the court five days a week and sometimes six or seven days in a week. There were weeks that Crissa would train seven days of the week, she was spiritually hungry and thirsty to fulfill her dream, vision, and hope. One day, she would be the star according to her vision and destiny.

Her love for basketball was purely love in action, she would never miss practice or training. Her drive was to always trained or died trying to train. All of this was happening to her, she was so inspired from the love of the game that was birth into her heart at the age of six by the Holy Spirit.

The bible taught her, love never fails, and you could see the scriptures energizing her during her training on the track and basketball court. She had to depend on her daddy at an early age to get from God what she needed.

Crissa believed, if she would act on what her daddy shared with her, somehow she knew it would come to pass. He remembers how she would watch and listen to what he said to make sure at least he sounds right or he is making some kind of sense.

Crissa would help her dad by listening very close, to make sure what instructions he was giving her about ball handling, was the correct way to handle and move the ball. She made sure that her dad got all of her input, because they were a team.

If she was going to get any positive results, she had to work together with her dad, he only knew about certain things about basketball. What great faith she had in God and her daddy even though they started out without a glue what they was going to do.

Crissa was very young with hardly any life experience, her heart was strong, obedient and trustworthy. She knew, everything would work itself out even though her daddy had no basketball training or professional skills.

Only God's love can discern and reveal to a child's heart, to be able to see her daddy heart and life. To be able to give him that support, comfort and assurance that everything is going to be all right. She kept training like an energizer bunny, just training, training, and training.

Her kind of training was being talked about by everyone in the city because of the love that she poured out of her heart and mind into the Susquehanna track and hills and the basketball courts throughout the city of Harrisburg.

Her daddy would like for you to travel with him, from his imagination concerning the place where Crissa was operating from on a daily base. Crissa had to be able to perform all by herself for hours on the track and court.

Her daddy would imagine that she was not alone, but she had a love companion that was in her heart and mind that empowered her every step she took and every time she touched the ball. He would imagine her talking with the Holy Spirit about how tired her legs and arms was, and the Holy Spirit would aid her.

He would imagine that she knew and understand that she had to finish the workout, the Holy Spirit gave her a dose of the anointing that would break all of her yokes. The Holy Spirit also gave her a shot of the anointing that would quench her thirst with the energy of the spirit.

God was moving all over her, inside out and outside in, she was living and training according to her dream, prayer, and spiritual sacrifice for the sport. The scripture spoke to her, she should give her body as a living sacrifice for basketball, holy and acceptable through prayer and fasting, which is her duty.

The Holy Spirit also let her know that she would not be like others who trained for basketball, she would be transformed in her basketball skills and training by her continued practicing. She would prove that the love of the game will open doors of opportunity and closed windows of negativity.

God opened another door for Crissa, to be able to go to the Five Star basketball camps for two years in the state of Virginia. In that state, God allowed her to meet Mr. Sylvester Clay, who offered his services for free, to train her how to develop a jump shot, which was a prayer that was answered.

Again, her dad was observing how God was answering her prayers and adding to her skills, and he was noticing how the both of them were getting more excited. She came to her dad and told him how she felt about God wanting her to do things spiritually.

He truly felt that this was one of those times to have a father-and-daughter talk. Dad began to go over how they were going to succeed with God's help, how the Holy Spirit was going to empower both of them to be able to get the things done that was needed for training and practicing for the next several years.

He shared more information that was based on their experience together with God, to help her try to become accountable to God for her-self, base on what she knows and have experience up to this point in her life of basketball.

He was only trying to help her to be responsible like any daddy would do to help his little girl and that was to encourage her to pray, fast, and read the scriptures on her own relating to basketball. He tried to express to her in the spirit of love, "if you want to be successful, then you are going to have to try to deepen your love relationship with God."

When he looked in her eyes and saw the seriousness and love for the game, he knew in his heart that one day she would receive from God a breakthrough for professional basketball because of her love for the game.

Those were the days and times that he saw the Holy Spirit cause a fire to burn on the inside and outside of her, like a light giving her the ability to be able to see basketball things in the hidden scene of the spirit of love.

It was like the Holy Spirit was revealing it to her while she was training and practicing. He knew, he was the trainer, but deep down inside of his heart, he knew that the Holy Spirit has taking complete control, it was reveal to him, this was the beginning of their separation of training and practice.

He was reminded by the Holy Spirit that he was only leading her to the water for independency, but God was showing him that the time is coming where she was going to have to drink and eat for herself. He was not sure; he could let her go because of his love for her.

In other words, all she would need from him was the opportunity to become more dependent on herself and the Holy Spirit. The time came where all he did was drop her off to practice and training and pick her up and take her home.

He was witnessing one of the most inspirational times in his journey, seeing his little girl growing up together with God's love in basketball, to be independently strong and responsible. This was the Jackson's family history in the making for daddy's little girl.

Crissa was able to establish that gift in her heart and out of her heart flowed the ability, talent, capability, and the power to train, practice, and play the game of basketball. The bible states that out of the abundance of the heart the mouth speaks and acts on God's love.

Crissa spoke life and destiny into existence for the success of a breakthrough of becoming a basketball star, because of the love of God. He knows that your child can use most of the things he mentions in this chapter to become whatever they want to be through love.

At this point in the chapter, it is very important that he shares with you that a lot of families do not know how to give or dedicate their child back to the lord. Remember, God will minister to the gift that he has put in your child to fulfill their destiny.

This is a very important fact and point; God's will be done for all new born babies. According to Romans 12:1, God tells you to give yourself and your children to him, none of you will be conformed to the negative nature of this world, you will be transformed by the renewing of the minds.

This is truly the parents' part of preparation for the mind, heart, and the spirit of your child. This indeed is one of the methods and procedures you can use to start preparing your child for their destiny and the future.

Your responsibility as parents is to make sure that your children are not deformed or conformed to this lost world of sports and the negativity it brings with it. It should be your number-one duty to protect and keep your son or daughter secure and give them a fighting chance in the world of sports.

Even if it appears that they are not going to make it, even when they grow up, one thing for sure and two you are certain, they will have the spiritual fundamental training that would already establish a love foundation. They will be given a fighting chance to be successful one day at a time on their journey.

These are the most promising spiritual facts and principles, they will give your daughter or son the promises of God's covenant of love, their love will grow by the very hand and word of God in the mind and heart of your children.

God said that he watches over every word of love that he plants and sows into your child, as well as yourself. His love words will perform the very thing that it was sent out to do, it will not return unto him void.

The point of all this, is for you the reader, to understand that the power of success in any sport is based on the love of the game. This love can't be fake, false, duplicate, or phony, it must be the real deal. In other words, you got to have true love for the game.

Please, do not get this twisted about the love that he's truly talking about, this love will cost you your life, he pick this time in the book to let you know, you have to be clear about how you are going to pursue the love of sport, as the little girl's daddy or mommy.

How much do you want this for your son or daughter? Remember, it is very important when God gives you a love gift for you and your child. Just remember, you must give the child back to God so he can organize their lives over time, especially when they are very young.

Remember, no matter how hard you try to give direction and training to your child; it has to come from God through our lord and savior Jesus Christ. If you want success for your child, then you personally got to have a relationship with God.

Your relationship with God will let you get God's plan for your child to be successful in life. You will have to talk to God about all of your plans good or bad. In other words, the bible says this kind only comes out through fasting and praying, so you have to spend time with God talking to him about you and your children future.

Also, you have to shut down your body physically by denying your flesh and sacrifice specific things that your body craves. The purpose, so your spirit can hear from God about what he is trying to communicate to you spiritually about your child and the sport.

Remember, if you truly love a sport with the love of God, you will be able to do exceptional, extraordinary, remarkable, and wonderful things, God's love endures, believes and hopes in all things for the sport of your choice.

You must understand that God's love never fails in anything, if you apply this principle in everything that you do, you will never fail at what you do. Your pursuit for the love of sports will come to pass while pursuing your dream and vision.

He wants all dads and moms to know, you will be able to discern love in your child during the course of your training and practicing the sport. Love is a discerner of the thoughts and intent in your child heart while pursing the sport of their choice.

This is one of the reasons why he wrote this book, so millions of sons and daughters around the world would start trusting the love of God in their heart while pursing the sport of their choice. God spends so much time trying to help them in their darkest hour while they are following their heart.

Another area that works through love is the five natural and spiritual senses, the senses can help so many people who like to play the sport of their choice and do not know how to operate in their five senses because of the lack of God's love for the sport.

If you been following his teaching about love, then you will know that everything a sport player says or does has to be accompanied by true love. Many people can't see, hear, taste, touch, and smell basketball or any sport.

This is not your everyday talk, he is sharing with you about not having the natural and spiritual senses, and the ability to train and practice while on the track and court. That's why he is sharing this spiritual truth so it can get way down into your heart and make changes.

Daddy really wants to help you to understand the truth about love, it states, if a little girl or boy wants to become great in the sports of their choice and the father wants to help them to be great, then both daddy and little girl or boy have to get the greatest gift of all time from God.

This true love comes from spirit realm and not the natural realm, it is God's love for the sport of your choice. Daddy is hoping that this information is making some kind of sense to you, he needs you to know in your natural understanding, you can't do this with your natural ability, you are going to have to get help from God and not the devil.

Daddy thought he would just make it plain and shame the devil. Things might appear like good and happy times without God, that is the deception of the enemy of your soul concerning sports. Things that the enemy produces are just temporary and for a little while, so don't be deceived about where the greatest gift of all time comes from.

Love has the power and ability to touch the ball, see the ball, smell the ball, taste and hear the ball from your heart. True love will help you to exceed normal and average skill levels in any sport you choose. This could be your window and door of opportunity.

He has been talking to you all this time about the gift, how it has the power to deliver you, he thinks you know exactly what gift he is talking about and he is going to leave it like that for right now. The things he found and discovered that other kids did not have in their heart is that gift.

You have to be convinced in your heart that love is not only the gift of God, but it is the power of God, and it is God. It also states, God is love, so, that must mean that love is God. Daddy is just trying to give you information that will support his true love story of daddy and his little girl.

This is a true love story, a story supported by the help of God the Holy Spirit, this story will reach over one hundred billion people and cause a love revival in sports around the world. If you can understand this concept, it could help you to receive the truth about God's love in sports.

Look at what the "Corona Virus has done to the world of sports and only the love of the game can put anyone back on track or on the court. People all over the world have been change about sports over time because of the Virus.

Remember the story of Egypt, Moses told God's people to put blood on the lentil post and the death angel would pass over. In other words, the blood represented Christ, it will cause the virus to pass over you, because God is love in blood.

The bible says, in the beginning was the word and the word was with God and the word was God. He has shared with you that God is love and God is the word, so, if you add the two together, you come up with the word of God is love!

Now, he wants you to travel with him in thought and understanding about the love word according to Hebrews 4:12 that states: "For the love word of God is alive and active. Sharper than any double-edged sword, it penetrates even to dividing soul and spirit, joints and marrow; it judges the thoughts and attitudes of the heart."

In other words, it is happening in your heart, love is revealing the game of basketball through training and practicing on the court and track of your choice. In other words, training or practicing in love will lead you and your little girl or boy to the final love frontier.

It is from your heart located in the soulish realm that is way deep down inside your body where God's love is deposit and stored. The things that love does inside of you will only enable you to be the best of the best sport player that you can be.

This information, you might want the Holy Spirit to help you understand by revealing the truth of the next statement that he is going to share with you. The love seed begins by verbally and physically depositing it on inside of the soulish realm to enter and deal with your heart.

That seed will cause changes to your mind, character, and personality, it will change your whole natural being to be able to think about loving the sport of your choice. True love will be able to receive from the Holy Spirit and build a love relationship with God and basketball.

The reason why all this is possible, it is God the Holy Spirit down inside of you that will be helping you, like he did daddy and his little girl. He will help you to learn how to work together in love in the sport of your choice.

Now, it is up to you to read and study about the love of God, so you can start your sport journey. The true purpose of this book is for the God of love to release you on your love journey to build a love relationship between daddy and his little girl or mommy and her little boy.

This love relationship will be for the rest of your life, that is exactly what love does, it draws people together. The bible states with loving kindness God have drawn you to him, with that same love he will draw you to your children and your children to you.

Did you know that the power of the tongue gives birth, by the words you speak out of your mouth concerning love? His little girl did the impossible and made it possible to succeed in her journey, she believed in the power of the tongue very strongly and the love you need to have for basketball.

It is so important that you have the spiritual ingredients from the scriptures if you are going to train your daughter or son. He has given you the spiritual recipe to be able to organize a spiritual plan, so you can get the job done.

Without God's plan of love, you will not succeed in developing the full package that you need for a love relationship to happen while you are on the journey. The scripture said, eyes have not seen and ears have not heard, neither has it enter into the hearts of sport players the things that God has for them who love their sport with the love of God.

Her daddy wants you to take a very good look at all the doors and windows God opened for her down through the years up to this point of her basketball career. God made a way for her to join the Niki Trick Team and this opened up her ability to strengthen her ball handling skills.

That's all it took for her to do was practice tricks with professionals. She got better and better until years later, her daddy told her that "God wants you to do trick as a part time job, just to earn some money and get exposure."

Daddy told her that she could do it while she was going through college, and she replied to him, "If that's what God want me to do, then he would make it happen." She also said that she would prefer WNBA before she would do tricks for a living.

Daddy knew when the Niki Trick Team made her a part of their team, they saw something great about her skills and wanted to capitalize on that during their shows. She noticed, as time was passing by, how her body and mind was becoming one with her drills. She was producing the skills with hard work and the anointing was on her like fire shed up in her bones.

All he knew was his little girl was on fire! Sometimes, she would train overtime by dribbling around the track. Her prayers that would kick in, and her faith in God every day at practice would kick off, she was seeing that prayer has changed everything about her ability to be able to perform at a higher skill level.

She was starting to give God the praise and glory when others would tell her how good of a ball handler she has become. Before that, she was always giving her daddy the credit as though he was actually developing her skills.

Her dad let her know, he was only a vessel being used by God to help his daughter who has tapped into the love of God for basketball by the power of God's love. Remember reader, the bottom line in this book is about the love of God only.

This love helped her to produce through prayer, fasting, faith, and trusting the process, she was always successful, when she depended on the Holy Spirit for every step of the way through love. God had a blessing for her to trust for success, and he gave it to daddy to give to his little girl.

Her daddy never been educated in training anyone in sports, he had to open his heart to God for guidance concerning the love training. He was only able to compare his experience in the ministry and military to train her for basketball.

Now, his love training that he had to endure when he was appointed and anointed as a servant by God, cause him to be chosen as a love vessel to serve as an evangelist, pastor, and teacher according to Ephesians 4:11, 12 is all he had to offer her at that time.

Daddy took that love training and began to establish prayer and fasting with her, he knew he could not do anything without establishing a love foundation with prayer and fasting. So, he started too fast and prays for the leading of the Holy Spirit.

Daddy knew, when he got to the track that God was going to deposit in him, what to do that made sense when it comes to basketball. It was basic love training, information that God gave to him too start the love journey of training.

One of the things the Holy Spirit brought to his attention, is what he learned from the streets while evangelizing to win souls. What he learned from the church service, is how to be faithful in his love character.

So, he was instructed by the Holy Spirit to take his little girl to the track so she could learn to dribble while jogging around the outdoor track. Then right after the track, he would take her to the outdoor basketball court so she could learn to shooted the ball.

As they continued the basic fundamental love training throughout the years, it became obvious through prayer and fasting that God added what she needed to do over time. He was now paying attention to anyone and everyone who dribble or shoot a basketball from all walks of life.

His ears, mind, and heart were open to learn about basketball like never before, thanks to the Holy Spirit who is the real teacher and revelator, who guided him and his little girl throughout the whole process to become students of the sport.

If he would see anyone dribble, shoot, or do any kind of workout for basketball, he would try to get knowledge and understanding from the Holy Spirit about what they were doing, especially if it could help his little girl.

During his love training in Bible College, he was taught to glean information and make it his own and that's exactly what he did for his little girl. Figuratively, he ate the basketball meat and spit out the bones, if that can be used as an analogy.

The Holy Spirit kept telling him that she needed repetition, to do it over and over and over again, so that's how he trained her to dribble around the track over and over again. She was building up to one mile, then two miles and he kept adding and would not stop for her and no body.

People were telling him that he was pushing her too much, and he needed to learn how to train professionally, but what the people didn't know and could not see, he was driven by the Holy Spirit and by her love to be the best.

He always tried to wait on the Holy Spirit to tell him when to add to the training and that worked like a charm for him. After a many years of working with the Holy Spirit during her high school years, things started to change in the workout.

The Holy Spirit told him to add to her work out steep hills to dribble up and down to learn how to dribble in different angles and for more control of the ball. He also found steep stairs for his little girl to run up and down, carrying the ball for touch and feel under pressure.

She loved the different things that the Holy Spirit was giving them down through the years, she started to look to the Holy Spirit for inspiration and opportunities for fancy tricks dribbling that would allow her to use both hands.

If she falls on the floor, she wanted to be able to continue to dribble without losing the control of the ball with either hand. She was learning for the first time to be able to control the ball with both of her hands

As he mentioned earlier, during her five-star camp experiences, he met a gentleman by the name of Mr. Sylvester Clay, known and called "Big Daddy," who offered his services unto God with no cost to teach her how to develop her jump shot.

Daddy did not have a clue how to teach her to do that, God kept the door open for her to travel with People-to-People Student Ambassador Program, travel with Niki Trick Team for four years, Five-Stars Basketball Camp for three years, Point Guard Camp for two years, AAU Traveling Basketball Organization for three years,

Elementary Basketball for two years, Middle School Basketball for three years, High School Basketball for four years.

God has blessed her with opportunities that established her future and relationship with him through basketball. Crissa trusted God process, she has given her best performance every step of the way, in so much, she told daddy that she would like to move to the state of Arizona for her twelfth grade year and when they got to Arizona, she was fired up!

She was so fired up that she said dad, I will train harder and go to church every week and read, fast, practice, I will train faithfully with you and the team practice. Now listen, she told her dad that she would not fail him or her team.

Daddy's first thought was he would have to provide his part throughout her training, but she was still showing her independency and the people in Arizona were beginning to pray for her gift of basketball. She was really maturing as time went on concerning her spiritual relationship with God and basketball.

Many of times, they talked about how the Spirit of God was going to help her basketball skills like nothing she had ever known. Daddy always explained to her how the Holy Spirit was going to develop and transform her skills as she continued to train and practice from the supernatural into the natural.

As the months were going by, she understood the revelation and insight that the Holy Spirit was giving her in her twelfth-grade year. She kept pressing her way for help from the Holy Spirit to build her love for the game of basketball. She also went to IMG Academy in Florida for one year, and four years of College Basketball.

When he looks back, all he could remember was her love journey of faith through love that enabled her to follow her heart, dream, vision, and hope that one day she would not only be one of the greatest female star basketball player of all times, but she would become a star for God and shine in the hearts of people all over the world.

CHAPTER THREE

DADDY BABY GIRL

W hen she was in her mother's womb, the father could not wait to see what his baby would look like, all of his babies were beautifully mixed with black and white with a very light complexion, but this baby came out with her father complexion and with the same color of hair and skin.

The baby looked like she had a whole lot more of Indian in her than the rest of the kids. He started out by calling her daddy's baby girl, and she would always blush like her sisters would do when he called them daddy's baby girl.

Daddy remembers how calm she was as a baby when they put her in her favorite baby swing, and he would push her back and forth, back and forth. He still remembers how she started moving around in her walker, and he would play and watch her get around.

As time went on, she started crawling around on the floor and he started crawling around with her and she would go the opposite direction and turn around to see if he was following her. In just a couple of months, she started to pull herself up on the couch and start taking steps, showing daddy that it is just a matter of time and she will be walking.

Because she had older siblings (Jay, five years old, Aleena, four years old and Marilyn three years old) who were almost one year apart, whenever they would go anywhere as a family, daddy would have to carry her, her mom would have to hold the hands of her other siblings.

Crissa and daddy, just like the rest, were becoming attached to each other. Now, he knew that she was different than her siblings because she always wanted to nurse on her mother's breast, and she always wanted daddy to hold her.

He knew that each one of his children wanted love to a certain point and then unattached themselves, but not her, she held on tighter and tighter and would not let go. She would not stop breast feeding until she was four years old.

She stayed up under her dad all the time when she was not playing, and he knew that school will be soon starting for her. So, her mother and father start suggesting to her that she could not continue to breast feed, and you should have seen her face.

She would still climb up on her mother's lap and start trying to open up her garment and try to get some breast milk. Nursing and holding her were her ways of being comforted and loved, which empowered her with the one thing that all people need, and that is love.

Now, school has started and dad started to take her to school and spend time in her class at least twice a week, and she would love it because she loves being close to her mommy and daddy. Now you have to understand that her mother was visiting her class as well.

She would always jump and climb on her daddy as a little girl after he would get home from work, then she would whisper in his ear, "daddy do you have any candy?" That was her favorite question growing up as his little baby girl, her siblings taught her the question.

He would tell the siblings that they could not get any more candy because they had enough. What they would do was teach Crissa this question, "daddy, can I have some candy?" knowing that he was not going to turn down his little baby girl who does everything right in life, so far.

Now concerning the siblings, they knew that if he gives candy to her, he would have to give candy to all of them as well, which was one of the rules in the home. If you give to one child, you must give to them all.

As a baby growing up, she is full of fun with all her toys and siblings to play with, going to the parks, recreation, swimming in the pool, the San Diego beaches and going for walks in the mountains was the love of her life.

CHAPTER FOUR

THE LITTLE GIRL JOURNEY

The journey included him taking her to the store at least once a week to pick out her favorite candy. He knew that was big time spending to her and she treats candy like adults treated money; she would treasure her candy by protecting and securing it at all times like adults protect their money.

One day, she asked the big question, daddy can you teach me basketball? He did not know what to say to her being only six years old, and that was the question that bonded them together for life like nothing he has ever experience in his life. For three hundred sixty-four days a year for twelve years, they were together.

Give or take a couple of weeks they were not together most of those years. They would get up in the morning, Daddy would fix her breakfast and make her a juice with fruit and vegetables, but it had to be sweet.

He would take her to school every day and pick her up, he did not want her to walk or ride a bus. He wanted her to know that he was there to take care of his little baby girl. He wanted her to know that he was committed being the advocate and security during the whole process.

After he would pick her up from school, he would talk to her about her classes and her grades while they were on their way to the track. When they got to the track, they would get all of their training equipment out of car and begin to pray, and when they were finished at the track, they would leave and go to the basketball court and do the same.

When he would take a look back at his humble beginning of fasting, praying before every practice, and training and talking to her about how he thinks God's is going help the both of them, it was just the way things got done in their new beginning.

The both of them knew nothing about training and practicing with no one to help them. Now you must understand that they were not wasting any time, they had developed a work and time schedule. He was learning to manage and she was learning to be managed, so they could have some type of order and routine that would not cause any problems with home, school and work.

They developed a list of the things they could do at the track and the basketball court, and as they grew together, they added other outdoor workouts in different towns. They became a team, partners, and working together to get the job done.

He set her down and explained to her how they needed to work together, and she was so happy that they entered into an agreement, she said, she was going to do whatever he asked from her, which would only be in her best interest.

This is a personal note from daddy stating, when you have a child look at you and tell you that they are going to do everything you ask them to do, this is good. His point is this, you need to know that this kind of trust and faith come from the love that you show them as a team or partner.

He knew then that they had just gotten closer and more bonded, now, he knows that they needed each other to fulfill her dream and reach her destiny. This was the point of no return, moving forward in the speed of love.

Then they decided that they should work out on the weekends, they had more time to expand the training to running up hills, dribbling the ball with both hands. They loved driving to another town that had steep hills to run, and she loved the fact that most players on her basketball team wanted to join her in her intense training.

Because he allowed them to train with her, she saw another side of her dad allowing her to reach out and help others like he was helping her. Their bonding became inseparable, and God was still knitting and binding them together not only physically, spiritually but mentally.

They started thinking alike, especially when it came to furthering the training; she began to incorporate her ideals and started to become independent in her work ethics. He started dropping her off at the gym and returns to pick her up, all she needed was transportation.

Later she started riding a bus from school to the gym and run the stairs at the gym, she had written down her own developed workout and drills. He only did her nutrition and her messages and pick her up after training.

He would just manage her by making sure that she had all of her equipment that she needed to do her workout. He began to look over the years they have been together traveling, to many different states for week's together, learning, discovering, and comparing their training and practicing to others that were training and practicing.

They have grown to trust and depend on each other to work together, and he watched her grow physical, spiritual and mental as a female baller. He watched her over the years take responsibility at home, school, and training.

The best love that she could offer her daddy was accepting her daddy as man with no training experience to train her. What he did before her eyes was to love her through the roughness, toughness, hard times, and good times.

Her dad would not quit while they were on their journey to stardom. He was so connected with her ability to be responsible, to love unconditionally, to understand him without limits, and to tolerate him under all kinds of conditions.

He decided to allow her to go to another state for her twelfth grade year to experience greatness and growth not by herself, but he decided that he was going to sacrifice his life by leaving his job and everything behind, including her mother who did not want them to leave.

This was another opportunity for them to bond on a different level like never before, so they started the journey traveling by the car her mother sacrificed, so they could have a dependable car to take them to a state that neither one of them ever lived in and bring them back home. Before them was their biggest challenge and adventure for the love of basketball.

They both wanted success so bad that you would think that the both of them were training and seeking the same thing. At this time in their lives, they have become one to the point that they got a one-bedroom apartment that was very nice.

It was her first apartment and they talked about her making this her apartment and he would show her how to pay bills, clean the apartment, and maintain the apartment as if she lived alone. So, they entered into agreement and for one year, that's what they did and she learned how to live and take care of her responsibilities and paid the bills with his money.

It was a tremendous building block time for her at the age of sixteen during her twelfth-grade year. After her practices, they would still train to advance her skills and experience in training for her last year in high school. Her school for a long time finally made it to the play offs at Arizona State University.

She finally graduated from Mountain Ridge High School in the state of Arizona. She found out about IMG Academy for her thirteenth year, got excited because this meant she would start another journey for them, but he could not go with her.

She knew that the time has come in their lives that they would go their separate ways, and all that he has taught, trained, prayed, and fasted for twelve years, plus her own personal experience, she would be able to make her own decisions and way without daddy.

This was a tough time for the both of them because he was used to waking up to served her, and she was used to waking up to be served as daddy's little girl. So, daddy's little girl went to Florida to do her thirteenth year at a "Professional Training Academy."

She was now getting all the professional training that she would need to develop her for college basketball. This was a great move towards her career. When she was finished at the academy, her mother and father drove down to Florida to IMG Academy.

Her father knew, he had to travel with her mother to IMG Academy to pick her up and drive her to Savannah State University to drop her off to her new college. This was like a dream come true for Crissa, but daddy knew he has come to the end of his journey with his little girl.

After about one or two months at Savannah State University, her basketball season was starting, and daddy decided that he needed to see her during her basketball season, which gave him a good reason to go to see her. That's exactly what they were both used to seeing, is daddy at the games.

So, he called her and told her that he was coming to stay for a month, and they were both excited, he made all the arrangements because he knew that he had been diagnosed with kidney failure, and he would have to start dialysis treatment with-in the next year, his doctor said.

He knew that this would be the only open window of opportunity for him to see her in action at her new school. Daddy's little girl finally made it to a D1 school with the possibility of moving on to a pro basketball team.

He got to spend a lot of time with her on campus and in her dorm with all visiting rights as a parent, and he never would have wanted to miss this opportunity. When it was over, he took with him home some of the most wonderful experiences that he had with his baby girl, especially visiting her dorm.

After about two weeks home, daddy got this important phone call from Crissa that she changed her mind and decided not to go through with her special projects of the things they were discussing. In a couple of months, he received another call from her that her situation changed because of her decision.

But still, she was daddy's little girl, and he had the greatest opportunity to be there for her in one of the greatest decisions she had to make in her life at that time. Daddy and his little girl growing up would always treasure this time in their life.

What does daddy's little girl mean to you? The way daddy understood, it is supposed to mean; a father or mother who loves his daughter or son unconditionally, absolutely, completely, entirely and totally would help them in the choice of their sport.

True love is what this book is all about when you have read all the information. A daddy or mother that is ready to serve their little girl or boy with love are parents that are ready to take the love journey of a sport of their choice.

Daddy's little girl learn to believe, trust, have faith, confidence, and depend on him, accepting him just as he is her advocate and supporter. Daddy's little girl becomes the person who obeys, submits, follows, does as she is told, comply with and abides by the things her daddy tells her about training.

As long as daddy is following the love of God, he is provided with inspiration and motivation to managing his little girl. He makes it his business to know that God gave him a little girl to care for on a personal note. When the right time comes, he must give her back to God so he can finish what he started.

Daddy knew, one day he would not be able to provide for his little girl any more of the love services for training for the game of

basketball. Daddy knew that his little girl would grow up to become this beautiful young basketball star.

He knows, God would be able to pick up the pieces for him to be involved with her. Daddy knew down in his heart that he had done all he could, and now she is in God's hand. This is a fact, that one day you got to let go and let God.

CHAPTER FIVE

THE FAMILY GIFT

I t was during the winter of 1989 a new gift was given by God to be born into the Jackson family, and everyone was excited about God's gift, especially Aleena and Marilyn. Jay wanted a little brother but had to settle with another sister to contend with in his home.

When she opened up her eyes and saw them for the first time, Daddy was thinking at that time, finally, she can see what she been listening to all those months. He figured it was a very good thing that she was not alone, but had siblings to comfort, support, secure, play, and show her a lot of love.

This was a very important time in the Jackson's family, they now had to work her into the love of the family. The Jackson's were a Godly family. What he means, he the head of the family, a preacher and teacher.

He is called (evangelist/pastor) according to the book of Ephesians 4:11, 12, and it was declared before she arrived that their home would serve the Lord Jesus Christ. This was no choice of her, she had no part in that decision, they taught her the ways of Christianity from a love position.

Not every child gets the opportunity to be raised up by the words of God's love in a home that serves the lord. When it came to the kids, he put a lot of restrictions and protection from what they called the world system of sin.

Even though Crissa would be exposed to the system, their responsibility as a family was to help each other to remember the teaching of the love of our Lord Jesus Christ when it comes to showing love. Time has passed, and she was growing up with a family of love who invested everything they knew about love in her as she was growing.

She was blessed to have a lovely birthday experiences with all of her siblings and some church member's kids. Her family was her support system for birthdays, Thanksgiving, Christmas, and the fourth of July every year.

As a family, the Jackson's established family traditions, hoping the children would keep it going or remember to establish their own family tradition. It was during the preparation for her birthday, mommy would allow her to participate in making the cake, and all the siblings would benefit from the party.

They did that so they would be able to go to each other's party just in case they were not invited out to any of their school or church parties that year. It was just another way for the Jackson's to have fun as much as possible every year.

The other was Thanksgiving, the children would participate in helping to prepare the Thanksgiving meal by shedding the cheese for the bake macaroni. They would want to help to set the table with the special gold silverware.

During Christmas, their mother established a tradition that would carry Christmas throughout the day to allow Crissa to open up only a few presents of her choice. Later that morning, she would be able to open a few more, and after Christmas dinner that evening, she would be able to open the rest.

It was designed to let all the kids celebrate all day with anticipation that it was not over yet. Another thing daddy taught them and that he was Santa Clause. He dressed up like Santa every year and they sat on his knees and he gave them presents.

The point of all this was about family spending times together, sharing love with each other, and making each other happy and joyful. He made sure that the love of God was deposited into Crissa like she has never experienced any place else on a holiday.

Because they lived in California, there was a lot of outdoors, and she loved that about her family because they would do everything together like going to the beach so many times a month and swimming in the pool that was right behind their home during their summer vacation blast.

She would go to the recreational parks throughout the city at least three times a week especially during the summer. Crissa started gymnastics when she was young and enjoyed it for a couple of years. The family would go to all the amusement parks throughout California whether near or fall.

When she was younger, they went to Knott Berry Farm, which is for little kids with great kid rides, and she would love to always go to that park. As she got older, they started taking her to Disneyland where it was for bigger kids.

She became so excited about those bigger rides that she completely fell in love with that park. At that time, they felt that they found a park that pleases all of the kid's, even mom and dad could have fun on some of the rides.

She always was excited about going to Disneyland because this park was not more than fifty miles away from their home, and they were about family having fun. Right around San Diego County, there was a park in lakeside called Scotty Park, and they would go to that park at least once a month, it has a lot of rides especially the bumping cars.

As she got older, they discover a new park and decided to take the whole church New Born Christian Fellowship to Six Flags Magic Mountain once a month, daddy was able to purchase a season family pass for his family.

The family entered into a decision together guaranteeing them once a month they would go to Six Flags for the whole season. They invited the church families and all the kids to share in the fun, the park was consider to be the biggest park in Southern California.

She was having the time of her life growing up in San Diego because she would have opportunities to go to Sea World and the San Diego Zoo. But sometimes depending on what school she went to; she would go to those places.

As a family, they would always go to the candy store to spend their allowance on junk food. He was called by the kids "the candy man" and consider being the junk food king. He opened the door as fun to create junk food junkies.

Crissa was require to take a bath every night, brushing her teeth before bed and the first thing in the morning. She also had to change her under cloths every day and do her homework and show it to her parents.

The Jackson's developed traditions in her that would last her for a life time. Another thing the family would do is go running throughout the city. They had a special mountain that they would run at least twice a week, and after wards, there would be a treat at Mc Donald's.

Also, they would ride their bicycles throughout the city of El Cajon and stop somewhere for a treat. Daddy would talk about riding on the streets, stopping at stop signs and red lights, and he would be leading and his son would be in the rear making sure that the girls would be okay.

It was times they would bond together because of the danger of being in harm's way while riding during traffic time around town and downtown. Not too long ago while the kids were still young, daddy was making good money for his family.

The Lord was blessing his family, and he figured he could purchase a complete wooded playground set with a clubhouse, swing, sliding board, and all the other features and benefits that came with the playground set.

It was one of the latest and newest technology on the market at that time, Crissa thought that all of that was brought for her because she was the youngest. His family had developed so much love for each other that they thought this would be a good time to travel as a family and tour the United States.

So, they talked to the school system and was told, in order to travel like that and miss school, you would have to homeschool them during the tour, and that exactly what they did. For one month, they packed up both of their cars and two siblings rode with mommy while the other two siblings rode with daddy.

Fortunately, Crissa rode with her daddy because she was the youngest, and the tour consisted of the history of United States, geography locations and places, math mileage and distance from state to state, English reading of their past, present, and future of their state, and tour of the history of slavery in her family.

The family loved the idea of taking the responsibility for each other, especially knowing that they were out in the open public driving throughout the United States, where people are preying on little kids as a means of occupation to support themselves.

So, they constantly informed the kids about holding hands and staying closed and watching out for each other at all times, and that added a little adventure and danger to keep their awareness and prudence awake and alert.

The family responsibility was to look out for each other, leaving not one person out of site, always watching for each other back, and helping out with anything and everything that you can. There were rewards along the trip for being responsible by helping and candy would be one of them.

He thought this was one of the greatest times in Crissa life, being with her family depending on each other. She was seeing her known world at that time with her family, which was building a security blanket inside of her heart.

This security would allow her to travel anywhere in the world, she has developed the love of family in her heart while journeying around the United States. When her family trip was over, it caused a bonding with the family that enabled all of them to pack their bags and move from California to the state of Pennsylvania.

She learned early that family is everything, and family love tides and love bonds can't be broken nor be separate spiritually. The Jackson's over the years have built a safe place that secures her love bonds that will take her all over the world.

Her connection would continue to build and created an internal love relationship with God that would establish her for the rest of her life. Her family will always be a love link that will stay connected to her for life.

Her love line is to become that love link that she will take to the world, the world will enjoy the love of God in her during the twenty-first-century. She has become a family love link that has extended herself to the world to share with other families lest fortunate than herself.

She has become one of the greatest love children of all times, when you meet her, you will see the love of the family coming out of her, that is all she knows from training, teaching, and loving throughout her whole process of growing up as "The Family Gift."

SECTION TWO

CRISSA THE LITTLE GIRL
PART 2
A DREAM COME TRUE

CHAPTER SIX

LOVE FOR BASKETBALL 1

A lot of kids like to start early in life to play basketball or a sport of their choice, they start messing around at the parks, school, gym, and maybe they got a basketball court at home. He feels that there is something on the inside that is driving them.

The reason he shared about God's love earlier, he wanted to introduce to you the secret behind the sport, and that is love. What's on the inside of you could be a touch of God love, it found you in a place in your heart, that you need the true love for the sport of your choice.

Not any kind of love, but the only kind of love that is true. He wanted you to know from the very beginning of the chapter, God is love and love is God and you need the love of God in order to come against the odds that are established and stacked against everything you try to accomplish in life, especially when it comes to sport.

Again, you have to know that God's love is the driving force or transportation that is able to take you from point A to B. What makes this book special is that he already revealed to you the secret for having success in sports.

You can't be new to this; you have to be true to this, daddy hopes when you are reading this book, you are asking God the Holy Spirit to help you understand everything that his love has done for daddy and his little girl. Not only does he pray that this book reveals to you what God is doing for him and his little girl, he has shown you what God is going to do for you and your little one.

He wants you to know that this book was designed with the help of the Holy Spirit of God, so the true love story of Crissa Jackson would produce the blessings and the power of the Holy Spirit of love. Throughout this book, you will be bless and given spiritual instructions how you can become successful by faith through love.

It was in the year 1996, in the month of June when Crissa was only six year old. He was taking the kids to the school park where they could exercise by running and playing ball, which was normal for him to do with them.

His son (Jay) wanted him to play ball with him, so he stayed and played basketball with him, and the rest of the kids went walking and running around the dirt track. From out of nowhere, he heard his daughter "Crissa" say, "Dad, can you teach me to play basketball?"

Now, she did not ask him "could you play basketball with me?" That question took him by surprise, because with his busy schedule, he knew that he did not have the time to teach or train anyone, nor did he have the skills or training, so he answered her with this, "you are a girl, too young and too small."

He told her very softly, that "you can't reach the basket even if you threw the ball up at the basket, you can't touch the net with the ball." So, he threw her the ball and she threw it up and it did not touch the net.

He said, "now you understand what dad means," and she replied, "I am going to tell mom that you helped Jay, but you will not help me." He knew that he would be guilty of discrimination, favoritism, and not showing her the same love that he was showing her brother "Jay."

Now, he was not training her brother "Jay," he was just playing around with him by passing the ball to him, so he could shoot. She knew just what to say to get the right response from her daddy. So, it was that day the love journey began for the both of them, but what he didn't see was that a love door and a love window like he had never known spiritually was opening up just for them to see the love of God.

So, he took a boys' basketball, which is heavier in weight than a girl basketball, at that time he did not know that girls had a basketball that was made just for them. So, he asked her to dribble with the boy basketball with the right hand and she did it.

She did a terrible job, so he asked her to shoot the ball into the basket, and she could not touch the net with the basketball. But that didn't stop her from trying over and over again, so he kept throwing her the basketball.

He was a little discouraged, but he gave her more basic drills, she was getting an attitude with him by giving him the baby face because he was not paying her any attention. Remember she was the baby, and she was good at baby winey.

She was good at breaking up her face until her daddy would do anything she asked him, so, he tried to discourage her by tying her left hand to her waist so she would only have one hand to dribble. You see, kids at her age dribbled with both hands at the same time.

So, for five minutes, he thought she would give up, but she didn't as he can remember. She was the complete opposite, she replied, "what next, daddy" as though the training between them had already started and he was only trying to find out how serious she was about doing the different drills.

So, he did the other hand, and she passed that discouraging test as well. So, he blind folded both eyes and told her to dribble in place, he wanted to see if she could develop a feel for the ball or maybe she would say, "Dad, this is enough."

Well, looking back at that first day, he tried to discover what she wanted to do did not happen, she was so excited that she asked him to teach her basketball. All she was doing was jumping up and down off the ground.

Here he was for the first time, given responsibility by the love of God that he never saw coming and had no idea what to do and where to start. When they were done after an hour of playing around with her, at the same time he was checking her out, only to discover that she was so excited that she said, "Dad, you are going to train me right?"

He looked at her, not having a clue what to do or say, he never done this before or ever thought that he would be training or teaching anybody about basketball. As a loving father, he told her yes, in his heart the love of God exploded with passion in him to help his daughter.

She was so excited, she started telling every member of her family that she was going to be trained by her daddy. Daddy felt and knew that something was different about her excitement, because of the sound of her voice rejoicing all over the house.

He prayed to God to help him, he did not want to fail her, while they were on this basketball journey. He remembered his teaching and training in church and bible school. He remembers his teaching, when a child discovered something that they really have a passion to do, get behind them and become there greatest advocate and support.

But this was different, she wanted him to train and support her, and he never experienced anything like this from any of his other kids. God spoke to his heart and told him to look at her heart, and for the first time, he saw the love of basketball.

It took several days for him see the love of God pouring out of her into him, he never felt that before from any of his children who wanted to do something so bad. "Crissa" was so excited; motivated about her training at the very moment he said, okay he will train her.

During this time in his life, the love of God was dealing with him about his love working through him, to help her to be able to train and practice at the high school track and outdoor basketball court. He knew, he was new to this, but God's love was drawing him to be true to this.

His faith was in a place where all things have to work together for him and her, he was going to support her like he has never supported anyone in his life. He knew this was his time to shine as her daddy, and he was not going to let nothing separate him from helping his baby girl.

As time move on, he knew in his heart, God was showing him about his daughter needs, who needed his time and love. He knew he could train her to practice, and she would develop good practicing ethics. He knew that if she could do the same thing over and over again every day of the week, she would get better and better.

He told her, "if you want to be a professional, then you need to train and practice as a professional." He knew that statement would give him the edge, she would agree to add more to her training and practice. That was exactly what he had in mind, he gave her more reps at the outdoor track and reps at the outdoor courts.

His secret was to energize her and not give up or quit practicing and training with her. He did not know that her love journey would start in the year 1995 and continue up until 2012 or after she graduated from college in the state she was born.

What he knew at that time, he really never trained anyone before for anything. Now faced with the greatest challenge that a father had to face with a daughter who wanted nothing less than God's very best.

What he is saying to you, you are reading this book, this is your season of divine intervention. This is a special time in every mommy and daddy's life where you must recognize what the child wants to do in life when it comes to sport.

Now is the time to get behind that child with all of the support and love that you can mustard up. "You want your child to be successful, true love will give you success like he did for "Crissa Jackson." This kind of success, thinking back, was not overnight, instead he asked God to help him all the time.

He asked God over and over again to give her something so she would be quiet and focus. Whether or not, it was basketball that she really wanted to do with her love. He thought back to that first day when she asked him for help, and he put her to the test to see how bad she wanted to be train for basketball.

That's all he needed to know from her, as they were looking for the eye of the tiger and hunger of the lion. He needed something to speak to him, and then a thought or saying came to him about how you can take the dog out the fight, but you can't take the fight out of the dog, and all his doubts were sorted out within 10 ten minutes.

Now you have to understand that he was called by God as a love messenger during this time, and she did not know that when she asked him to do such a thing. She was really helping him to enter into his love dispensation of learning how to love God and everyone else, and one day he would be called the writing evangelist who writes books about love.

Immediately, he began to establish a method of training every day at the Grossmont College track in California, the Holy Spirit show him what to do there that would help her. Before he could establish her workout and training, he had to do time management with his job, ministry, and family.

He began to put time on everything, he had to have order in his life to teach and train his little girl like a good daddy and not neglect his other responsibilities. He was going to please his little girl by establish order under God through love.

The spirit of God led him to go to the track at Grossmont high school and then take her to the outdoor play ground with a basketball court. Everything was going to be done outside because, he could not find anything else at that time that he could afford.

He was able to buy her two 28.5-inch girls' basketballs, and she would dribble around that track one time with her right hand, another time with left hand. Now you have to understand that he had to tie the hand that was not dribbling the ball around the waist, kids that age are not able to dribble with one hand.

Again, she would do it with the other hand. Then she would work on both hands by dribbling two balls around the track. Now, the good thing about the track when it came to dribbling, the track had lines going all around the track.

The Holy Spirit told him and showed him to have her dribble the ball on the lines (ball on the line and feet off the line) and dribbling the ball right by her side all the time. That would establish the control of the ball, so she won't lose the basketball.

This training went on for months, and one day someone told them that there was a trying out for girl's youth basketball. At this time, she was only seven years old, and for the first time of her life, teams for little girls at Grossmont High School were starting that summer.

He told her and she became so thrill, she started to train with more commitment, dedication, and concentration. Up until this time, there was nothing for little girls' basketball, especially for elementary school, so for them, this was a miracle.

Now when he thought back when he needed a place to train, he did not know that there was going to be a girls' youth basketball league starting at the high school where they were training. He was very proud of the progress she was making at the track and court.

He knew that he would be able to tell whether or not she really wanted to trained and play the game of basketball for the first time, when he plugged her in to girls youth basketball. This would reveal the truth, nothing but the truth, for the love of basketball.

He knew, he would be able to measure her training and practicing when she started playing with others girls on the basketball court and when she played against other teams. You got to know this, there were not many little girls at the age of seven that were practicing and training for basketball in her area like she did.

Finally, the day had come for try outs and they were there in the building for the first time and there were so many little girls trying out that they were able to get at least 8 teams. His daughter "Crissa" had never seen so many little girls about her age wanting to play basketball, you could see the excitement all over her face.

So, they had all the girls line up and began to count to ten over and over until every girl had a number. That's how the teams were developed by the number, and whatever number your child was, that was the team your child was on.

She hesitated for the first time by saying she wanted to leave, and he asked her, are you nervous and scared?" She said yes daddy, she also said, "she is the smallest girl here." He started looking around and found another girl who was smaller than her and pointed her out, and she seemed to feel a lot better quickly because she wasn't the smallest girl.

Then he reminded her that she was the best girl basketball player in there and her whole-body language changed and he knew that she was more than ready to show off her skills to everyone in the building. After he made that encouraging statement, he could see how excited she was to play the game with other kids, like she had never experienced before.

This was her first time to ever play with a team and demonstrate what she knew and could do on the court. This was a special time for her because she was on a team where she could display all the hard work that she was putting into to be one of the best female point guards in the world.

She ended up on the team with a coach that would always see her working out, he would acknowledge her working out at the track and about how good she was doing at the track working out before she was on his team.

Her coach knew she could dribble, immediately made her the point guard because he would bring his daughter to work out at the school and see her dribbling around the track. Because of her practicing dribbling and shooting the ball every day, she was more than ready than dad could ever imagine.

She was able to dribble the ball with either hand, and at close range, she was able to put the ball into the basket. Her team went on to victory that year because of her ball handling skills at an early age. The next year, she went to try out and was on a team, and she came to her dad and said, "dad, I am going to be a star, and I want to named myself star."

She went on to name the team star that she played on, and her dad was made the coach of the team. She went on to do everything as a star, even her email address was change to star as she got older. From that experience, he knew something was about to break loose, so he increased her workout to crossover, through her legs, and around her back and dribble from side to side.

Every day she world go with her daddy after leaving school, to the track to dribble and then to the playground to practice her layups, bank shots, and foul shots. He noticed that his little girl was connecting the gift with her love for basketball.

In San Diego, California during the '90's, there were no elementary girls' basketball teams at any elementary school until you go to high school. So, he had to look throughout the county of San Diego to try to find an elementary school that had a girl basketball program, but he could not find one in the county of San Diego.

Everyone was beginning to talk about her skills everywhere she goes, he encourage her to carry her basketball with her to school, church, or the park to practice dribbling when she had time. She always listens to her daddy when he made sense.

She had a special assignment to carry her basketball wherever she goes because it would give her the opportunity to practice bouncing and controlling the ball everywhere, she carry the ball with her as part of her secret mission training.

To eat, walk, run, talk, sleep, and dream with the basketball in her hands was the memo of special ops training that he assigned to her, she would become one with the ball. It has been a few years now, and he has never witness anyone who has been more dedicated, committed, loyal, and faithful to basketball training and practicing like her.

When she was training and practicing to learn basketball skills, take note please; one of the most exciting things about the love of God, is when true love is operating through you, there will always be growth.

In other words, if you love the gift like you are supposed to, then there will be a responsibility in your heart, to release the love of basketball in your training and practicing that will demonstrate that you are not only a good steward of the love gift but you are the love gift.

When you become a hard worker of your gift, it will show that you are thankful, appreciated, and you treasured the opportunity to display your love for the art and science of basketball like no other baller on the planet earth.

He knew and understood spiritually, that it took the love of God to operate through her to be able to display that kind of love in order to produce the results that was needed at that time in her life. Because of dedication, commitment, loyalty, and faithfulness to train and practice, she was able at a very young age to become one of the best in the county.

He began to think how blessed he was to have someone like her to represent the family with such love and passion to learn about the game of basketball. But when it came to basketball through the Holy Spirit, dad was beginning to understand where her love for basketball was coming from, and he began embracing her with that same love, so they both could have the same common love ground.

He was beginning to believe that he had discovered a star, who was showing everyone that she is star material and that she was in the making of something very special and big in world of basketball by the Holy Spirit.

He did not have to worry about practice anymore, she was waiting on him, and he knew that because of her excitement that she had every day, tired or not. He would pick up every day after school, and her homework would be already done. What does that tell you?

She was an honorary student every year, and he told her that if her grades would fall below a certain average, she would not be able to play ball. Thank God that never happened, and he believes that she was one of those kids that did not like school, but only wanted to trained and play basketball.

It was the love of basketball that drove her every day of her life, and all he had to do was keep her routine fresh and exciting, so she would grow in her areas of skill from one level to the next. Nothing could stop her or get in her way; she was focused with her eyes wide open looking at the prize.

You have to agree with him, children can be your biggest surprise and you not know it. When you step out by faith and believe that your child can do all things through the love of God, nothing can separate you or your child from pursuing the dreams, vision and hope that is in their heart for breakthrough.

You have to know your child and the love that is driving with in them to be the best they can be every day for the rest of their lives. To have that fight in you, to never surrender nor be taken prisoner by anything that would discourage or try to defeat either one of you from the greatest opportunity that only comes once to most daddies and their little girl in one life time.

So, mommy and daddy, this is the time to step up to your child and step out by faith through love and command and demand that greater is the love that is down inside of you that will help your child to be drawn to the game of sports or any other life drawing opportunity that would give them success.

In her third-grade year, he moved his family back to Harrisburg Pennsylvania into the Susquehanna Township District, and the only thing that was on her mind was "when basketball is going to start?" This was the first time she ever had an opportunity to play for an elementary school team.

This was one of those times she couldn't wait to show her basketball skills, she have been working very hard every day developing her basketball skills in California. During this time in Pennsylvania, she was talking about WNBA and how she wanted to play professional basketball.

He told her, that "this means that you have to start training like a WNBA if you are thinking about playing in the WNBA. When you change your mind to think like a WNBA, then you are to think and train and practice like a WNBA."

So, he began to intensify her workout by having her to run a lot of sprints, dribbling one and two balls. Dribbling up bleaches and dribbling around the track for miles. Her workout was increased to two and a half hours a day to build power and strength.

He took her to the track first to build her legs and develop her handles, and when he would finish, he would take her to the basketball court to work out on the basketball drills. Now remember, his mission as she got older was speed and endurance.

He developed drill skills for the track and the gym, they were written down so she would have a guarantee written workout for every day. As she got stronger, he made the workout harder with her permission and agreement.

She was having the fun of her life playing basketball in elementary school and she was making new friends that would come over her house and practice with her and spend a night. She was beginning to live her basketball dream, while in elementary, playing her little heart out to do the best she can.

Everything with her was basketball, and everyone loved that about her. She was able to do things with the ball that girls her age was not able, not even the boys. They would look at her handles and always complimented her, how good she is as a ball handler, and she would just look at them with a hidden grin on her face.

He was so proud of her, but he knew it all came by hard work, training every day and not taking a break. Also, he knew that this was a beginning of something new, fresh, extra ordinary, and refreshing for her and him.

This was an important time of her life, she started to prepare herself for middle school, and there were others girls who were asking her if they could work out with her, they wanted to work on their basketball skills.

She would ask him, and he would say, "yes, it is okay for them to train with you," and that really helped her to be a happier baller, the girls at her school now wanted to train with her. One of her favorite players that could do most of her drills was Cadea Ruth.

This was a breakthrough for her up until now; she had been working out and training by herself for years. He could see the loneliness and tiredness that was gripping her and how she kept going no matter if she had to do it alone.

He knew, she was special and God was with her all those years and it was love that was her driving force. From the third grade to the six grade; she matured physically, mentally, socially, and spiritually. At the age of ten, she was going into the sixth grade.

Her physical condition was so good that she could run and dribble for one hour and a half. Her legs were strong, and her arms and shoulders were strong and tight. She mentally was strong, because of her skill, talent, and time she put into her workouts.

She was very positive and sure of her skills when she was playing as a point guard in her games. She had inspired a lot of her team players to train with her and spend time fellowshipping over each other's houses.

She never missed church and was always praying during the training and after the training. Another reason this was a special time in her life, she started to understand why she should eat right and get her proper rest for her body.

She was growing up in the world of girls' basketball like he has never known or experienced before with any of his kids. She was learning the game that she loves so much, and he was very excited because she was not that six-year-old that he started with four years ago.

Three hundred and sixty-five days for four years, give and or take a week of two, she did not believe in taking a day off. Her day was not like other kid's day, she would carry her ball to school, and she would do her homework during lunch time.

Any time she got a chance; she would leave from school and go right to the track and later the basketball court to train and practice. She would go home to eat, shower, and get a massage while in bed. Every day would be the same routine for her, and anyone who follows her knew where she was, because of her same daily routine.

Up to this point, she would only be allowed certain things to motivate her, and he used those things every time he could to get her to do more and to reward her for doing the impossible tasks or drills. One of the things that she loved was getting money for doing extra workout.

She would also suggest extra work for candy and not just any kind of candy, for she loved herself some Mexican candy that I purchase boxes when I flew to California. She had this special steak house that she would love to go to at least once a month, and that was her incentive for sticking to her schedule every week of the month.

She also received body massages every week depending on where her soreness was giving her problems from her mother and daddy. He noticed, she was turning into a female basketball machine that was starting to need fine tuning to be able to train harder, longer, and smarter.

Her mother and father knew how to massage and together they would take turns massaging her especially before she goes to sleep or a game. He knew that there were organizations that were training girls' basketball and he could not afford it.

He thought she might be missing some things or needed to do something different, so he decided to get her involve so she would not miss out on anything that God has for her. Everything was coming together for her during her sixth-grade year.

She was invited by the Student Ambassador Program to travel to Amsterdam capital of the Netherlands to compete against other teams. She returned home as a true winner and received the MVP for the hard work she has done in the Netherlands.

Her school team won the championship again that year. She started to get involve in AAU Girl Basketball Organization in the state New Jersey during that year right after school basketball. That was a very tough year for her because she had to be driven at least twice a week from her home in Harrisburg, Pennsylvania to the state of New Jersey.

Her parents had to make that drive taking turns driving up after work each night and when they return home; she had to take a bath, be massaged, and get up on time to be taken to school and be ready for training the next day.

Because she wanted to begin to try out basketball camps, he took her to the Five-Star Girls Basketball Camp that summer down in the state of Virginia after she graduated from the sixth grade. During the seventh grade, her basketball team won the championship again, and during that summer, she went to the same Five-Star Girls Basketball Camp in Virginia.

But this time, it was different because she had been there before, and she just knew what to do because of the prior year training camp. All the girls and coaches would complement her for being so young and able to run games with the older and bigger girls because of her ball handle skills and shooting ability.

She was having the basketball blast of her life, and before his eyes, daddy's little girl was growing up into a star just like she said she would become. He was so full of joy, and everyone could see that because they were telling him how good his daughter was, especially a gentleman by the name of Sylvester Clay, but everyone called him Big Daddy.

He was a very kind man, and he invited Mr. Jackson out for lunch one day during the Five-Stars Basketball Camp meeting, so he accepted. While they were having lunch, he offered his help as a business CEO, and a former college basketball star.

Mr. Clay said, God wanted him to offer his service for free to train her how to form her jump shot, and he accepted immediately his invitation. So, he introduced her to him, and when the both of them were driving back after the camp, daddy told her of their invitation, and she got excited, knowing that she was going to be trained how to form and shoot a jump shot.

During that week of training at home, she asked her dad, "when are we going to start the training with Mr. Sylvester Clay?" He told her that Mr. Clay wanted them to come up to spend a day and stay overnight in a hotel that he was providing for them. Again, she was thrilled because people were taking interest in her and wanting to help her.

He took her to the hotel in Virginia, and they stayed at the Hilton hotel. The very next day, Big Daddy took them to a basketball court, and Big Daddy trained her for a couple of hours starting under the basket and working out to the foul line.

Mr. Sylvester Clay, known as "Big Daddy," suggested that they called him that and they did. He taught her how to hold a form by keeping her arm in an L shape, and only moving her wrist to shoot the ball as far under the basket as she could for ball control.

He was teaching her to move slowly out from the basket to the foul line and taking only small steps at a time. Then later, he went on to show her the jumper and by teaching her the form of how to bend those knees and come straight up from the ground using the feet to push up and releasing the ball from the fingers by way of the wrist.

Big Daddy told her at the end of the training, you got to practice the forms from the beginning under the basket to the jump shot outside where the foul line was all the time. He told her to incorporate this training into her gym work out, and when she comes down again to Richmond Virginia in three months, he wanted to see some improvement.

In three months, he looked at her and was satisfied and went over and corrected whatever was needed. This was a very important time in her life, she knew if she could learn the proper form, how to shoot that ball it would enhance her skill and her game.

She also knew that she has never been taught the proper form to shoot and the proper form to shoot a jump shot. After this, Daddy knew nothing could stand in her way of her handles and her being able to pull up with the jump shot in the air.

She was ready to train harder on those two together to produce one of the most effective packages that a female basketball player has been able to do. She knew that perfecting these skills would make her basketball game armed and dangerous.

After winning the championship in her eighth-grade year, she was now facing the challenge of her life and that was high school girls' basketball. The only thing she had in mind was starting on the varsity team only, being in the ninth grade.

Another thing took place in her basketball life at the end of her eighth-grade year when she went to an event at the high school that she was going to attend in one year. The high school was having a team of men called the Nike Trick Team.

So, he told her about this event, and she said dad, "I want to go to see all my girlfriends and the basketball team," not knowing that she was to be introduce to the game of her future. So, he took her to the show, and when they got there, she saw some of her friends and was a happy camper.

When the show started, she was staring at the show, and as soon as they did one trick, she exploded, and the more tricks they did, the more excited she became. She replied, "Dad, did you see that? They are really good."

So, she took her own ball and began practicing the same tricks while Nike Trick Team was performing. That night, they picked her out of the crowd to be involved in the show like they always did with the little kids. Because of her height and she looked like a little girl, they picked her out to see if any of the kids could do their tricks.

That night was the birth of the "Thirteen Female of America Harlem Globe Trotter," and nobody knew then that the Harlem Globe Trotters was one of her destinies, not even her. She was so excited about being picked, she tried every trick they asked her and nailed most of them.

Wow he said, he has never seen her so happy about the tricks the Nike Trick Team was performing. She spun the ball on one finger with one hand. She rolled the ball across her neck to her hand on both sides. She tossed the ball in the air and caught it on her neck for a little bit, and "Wow," he said to himself, "this girl got trick skills."

In the back of his mind, he kept wondering how she was able to do some of those tricks, he began to think, when did she have the time during training on the track or practicing on the basket? This reveal to him that his little girl is gifted or she can learn very quickly.

Then he began thinking and trying to remember where she had the time to practice those things and it came to him while she was carrying her ball with her everywhere. She was a natural baller, and he couldn't wait to see what the future had in store for her.

He was beginning to see her get more involved with different kinds of basketball skills in her life. First, the Nike Trick Team added her to their team to travel the United States; she also, traveled with the People-to-People Student Ambassador Sport Program to Amsterdam.

She joined the AAU association, point guard camps, and finally she grew with ten girls who were working out with her every day, hot or cold, and if it would rain, they would all have to go indoor to a gym to get it done.

At the age of ten was a new beginning of new events taking place in her life like she had never known or experienced before. First, she was accepted by the People-to-People Student Ambassador Sports Program after applying and giving them a C D Tape of her basketball skills.

They were interested in her because they wanted her to travel out of the country. That meant for the first time, she would have to apply for a pass port in order to travel out of the country of the United States.

After meeting all of their requirements for the People-to-People Student Ambassador Sport Program, she was now ready to travel to see the world for the first time. He asked God what could this mean for her being so young and to be able to travel so far, and he replied that this is the beginning of her destiny.

He could not see what God was talking about regarding her traveling all over the world in the future, especially in the beginning of her training and practice. He stay focus on the basics and made sure that she was practicing repetition.

CHAPTER SEVEN

TRUE LOVE FOR
BASKETBALL 2

During that same period of time in her life, she got involve with two AAU teams, the first AAU team, her mother and father had to travel to another state in order for her to play. This team was considered to be one of the best teams in that state, and she wanted to play very bad, because they were considered very well and she wanted to run with the best only.

They contacted the team about the date for tryouts and they took her and she made the team. She had a blast competing with other teams in that state. AAU teams are considered the best players in the state battling against one another.

The second AAU team was located in the same county she lived, and again she had to play against other teams that had very good players. There was one team that she was so excited about because there was a girl that was good just like her and could play the point guard position and her name was Mona.

She liked Mona so much that they became friends before that season was over. She told her dad that Mona was the first girl who could play the game like her. During her three years at the Susquehanna Middle School, her workout crew grew up to 10 ten girls.

Girls from other schools would ask her if they could join the work out crew. The parents would give ten dollars a month if not a week to dad, and he would give it all to Crissa, because she would help them to endure the training.

It was a free will love donation, and he would let her have it because she knew that her job was training every day, because pay day was coming in a while. But he knew the most important thing about the girls was that she had other girls wanting to succeed in basketball, and they wanted to do it with her.

He could tell that she was one happy camper, the other girls wanted to be like her skillfully in basketball. She became the most popular girl in her school as a female player and because she not only was selling candy in school, but she had a candy business with established clientele at school.

She had students that would tutor her for free by helping her with her homework. Things were looking very good for her, he started going to her school by appointment to have lunch with her once a week to check on her to see how everything was coming along, and he was impressed.

Over the few years while in Pennsylvania, she became very popular in school, she was always invited over to the girls' sleep overs, and she would do the same in returns. She was living the dream because of good, hard, consistent work outs ethics that she would do every day.

Everything was paying off for her, the people in her city were talking about her skills and basketball talent. She was often asked if she would consider going to other schools that have a better girls' basketball program.

But at this point in her life, her friends were everything to her, and she wanted to play with them and be with them all the time. For years she would train alone and practice alone in California and Pennsylvania.

When she had the opportunity to have other girls participating in the training and practice, daddy knew in his heart that she would not be lonely anymore, and that was a spiritual breakthrough. He would like to make this note to you, love has the power to draw people into your life that wants what is practical and real.

Crissa is now living the Middle School basketball dream, many little girl would have embraced, if they had the opportunity. So much was happening to her every year and that was good for her because all her hard-working ethics was paying off before she graduated from Middle School.

When it became time for graduation from Middle School to High School, she was ready. He wants you to know what this meant to her, for her to be able to graduate to big girls' basketball league, was the bomb. Since she was a little girl, she would plan to get to high school girls' basketball and make the varsity girls basketball team in the ninth grade.

She was so motivated, inspiring, and excited, waiting for the tryouts, and when the tryouts were finally there, she went and did everything that was asked of her and nailed it. She made the varsity team, and she was a happy camper, knowing that everything she worked so hard for has paid off.

Now was time to get back to work, she knew that she had successfully reached another goal towards her dream and vision. She couldn't wait to start playing for the varsity team, but during the wait, she continued her routine work ethics by training and practicing more intense than she ever did before.

Four things were happening in her ninth-grade year that made her excited about playing for the high school varsity team. She kept traveling with the Niki Trick Team, she started to play with her dad's AAU traveling team after school basketball season was over.

She had a California friend named Jonathan Pascal, who was about the same age as she was, who loved basketball, was coming for the summer to spend time with her. Her ninth grade was amazing because she was now experiencing what she had already prepared herself for, and that was to be the best girl basketball player that her school had ever witnessed before.

She was very surprised to hear that my daddy's long time dear friend, Dr. Forrest Pascal, was going to send his son Jonathan to visit her for the summer. He knew Jonathan could play basketball, and being a boy, he would help sharpen her skills as a girl.

So, the time came when Jonathan arrived, and she was totally excited. She was having fun every day after Jonathan arrived and they went everywhere together, playing basketball, enjoying one another, and this joy and fun continued for the whole summer.

All dad did was video almost everything they did, so one day his father and mother would see the video. Jonathan returned home in California, and because of him, she grew stronger over the summer, drilling and playing with Jonathan.

Now that Jonathan had returned home, her confidence was high, her faith in herself was strong, and she was ready for basketball season, because she was in very good shape and tip-top condition. It seems to him that she couldn't contain herself.

Her training was more intense than it had ever been before. She was beginning to change her workout to more personal training on every part of her body. She started weight training for her body on her own time and still was able to manage everything else.

She was more than ready for her ninth-grade high school bas-ketball training after school. Her team had to run around the track for three miles to loosen up, and she would always finish as one of the top three or five on her team.

During the indoor drills, she would always finish as one of the three or top five. Crissa knew that conditioning was fifty percent of the training and she was in very good shape and the coaches saw how strong she was physically and assigned her to the varsity team immediately.

She had a fantastic basketball season, and during her first year in high school basketball, she was shown on TV several times on some of the sports news channel. She was even interviewed by one news channel out of York, Pennsylvania.

She had a fantastic year, but the basketball program that was installed was not the type of program that could further her basketball career, so she moved into the city of Harrisburg into her dad furniture store business just so she could get into a school that had a better program.

He was just one of those kinds of daddies that would do whatever it took to further his little girl's career. They moved and lived in the furniture store for over a year before she could live in a normal home in the city.

After converting part of the property of the furniture store into a two-bedroom apartment, she lived under those conditions for at least one year. Could you imagine being thirteen years old and subject to those conditions just to play basketball?

During this time, she started going to the Harrisburg High School and started playing for their girls' varsity basketball team in the tenth grade. The reason why she moved into the city of Harrisburg was to have a better basketball program and better basketball team.

Daddy knew she had to have the best because all she had was him, and he knew she needed more exposure. The Harrisburg High School girls' basketball team was winning most of their games and was able to the go to the finals that year.

She was having a fantastic season at that school. She was picked to be one of the "Big Fifteen" in the district, and that was a big thing in the State of Pennsylvania. That same year, she was interviewed and was put in the newspaper in the sports sections.

After basketball season in that same year, she ran for the high school track team, which she discovered that anything outside of basketball was a wear and tear on her mind and body. As of today, she still remembers the problems she had with the Harrisburg school, how they fought physically too much and there was just too much drama all the time for her to continue to go to that school.

So, she requested to be transformed to a school called Sci Tech, which was a math-and-science school program that accepted her into their program, and she immediately started their school and was still able to play basketball for the Harrisburg High School girls' basketball program.

She loved it, she was still traveling with the Nike Trick Team, doing her tricks and having so much fun. He remembers, when she had a show at half time during an NBA game with the Boston Celtics, and the Niki team would come out on the middle of the floor and start doing tricks without her.

Then they would pick out lots of kids, and she would be one of them because she was part of the show as their secret show girl. They would ask a few of the kids to do tricks, and some of the Nike men would spin the ball and put it on the kids' finger.

Being that Crissa was small in stature like the rest of the kids, everyone in the audience did not know that she was part of the Nike show. Her act was to snatch the ball from the hands of one of the Nike team members and begin to spin the ball on her finger, and the crowd would go wild.

Crissa would throw the ball up in the air and catch it on back of her neck, and then they would give her another ball to dribble, she dribble two balls at the same time while the audience was clapping and yelling at her performance.

Then the Niki Trick Team would send all of the kids back to their parents, but Crissa, they would acknowledge her as being the secret girl weapon on their team for the show. Crissa was all blown up with joy.

Then they would all bow together at the same time as to identify her as part of the team and leave together. After the show, she would sign autographs, and you could see the excitement and joy on her face while she was signing her autograph.

Every show, she was getting stronger and more skillful with her tricks. Another thing happens during her tenth-grade season at Harrisburg High School, she established a record at Harrisburg High as shooting the most file shots at one time (ninety-nine straight made shots made her the all-time record holder), and still today she holds that record for the girls' and boys' basketball program.

Right after the tenth-grade season, she was ready to travel with the AAU Traveling Team, this team she been training with for several months. These were hand-picked girls by her and daddy, they wanted to have a strong team.

She had a long-time friend throughout elementary school, middle school, and high school named Cadea Ruth whose mother was a part of her training since elementary school through high school, and that was about six years and counting.

He talked to Cadea's mother (Thanayi Ruth) about creating a basketball team, and she thought it would be a good ideal to put together a team. So, Mrs. Thanayi Ruth became one of the coaches, and Mr. Eddie Ruth became the sponsor for the team uniforms only.

The agreement that was established with Mr. Eddie Ruth was he provided the uniforms, and the team would become responsible for passing out his business flyers. The team agreed and got busy and passed out thousands of his flyers, and Mrs. Thanayi provided those uniforms through her husband.

The team was ready to compete as an organized AAU team. He was the head coach and was traveling all over the Pennsylvania area until they were in the final competition. The team was very happy and successful because they finished at the top with the best players hoping to take home the number-one trophy.

One of their coaches got kicked out of the game because she was the team cheer leader who was on the side line cheering about a lot of things that offended one of the officials, but that's was okay because they were in it to win it all or go home for trying.

It was Crissa eleventh-grade year, and she was facing one of the greatest challenges of her basketball career. In her eleventh-grade year, she again went to the playoff with Harrisburg High School with only two games left to be state champions.

Believe or not, they lost to a team that she thought the coach did not know how to play her, she was truly excited and motivated to win that game. That was a good year for her because she got to play her heart out to discover that her basketball coach had favorites.

He knew, talking about coach, that Crissa was disappointed when she played the sixth person. She figured the coach's method of playing his favorites cause her team to miss out on a great victory during the state playoff. Crissa was faster, quicker, stronger and her endurance was very good. She was prepared her whole basketball career for this challenge of stardom.

That was one of the reasons why her dad was thinking about removing her from Harrisburg High School basketball team, he felt this was her time, at the greatest basketball moment in her life, she was ready and capable to take on the challenge and win. He felt that she was not given her chance of stardom, win or lose.

She work hard for many years, waiting for the opportunity to show under pressure that she truly is a winner and not a loser. When she realizes that she would be the sixth girl, she knew that she was overlook at a crucial time she was needed to produce stardom.

Now, he had shared with Crissa, how it would be best for them to start looking for her a school for her twelfth grade year because everything she had work hard for led her to the final chapter of her basketball journey.

She needed to be with a high school where she could finish strong. Everything was going the way she wanted it too, she never stop working out even though they were looking for another school. Matter of fact, her work ethics became her first priority.

She created her own routine and scheduled her own workouts according to her time management with school and everything. She would go to school at Sci. Tech and catch the bus to the YMCA and start training before he even got there to oversee her practice.

Five days a week, she was at the YMCA doing what she does best, and that was making magic with her work ethics. No matter how much work she would do at the gym, she would let her daddy take her after the gym workout to run upstairs and dribble up steep hills in Steelton Pa.

He would have her run up and down the stairs during her training at the YMCA, if there was enough time. Everything that Crissa did depended on how much time she had to get it in before she needed to get home to eat and sleep.

During the end of her eleven-grade year all she could think about was how the Harrisburg High School coach played favorites, with his senior players. She felt that it cost her the championship title, and she deserved more as a star player.

She brought it up again about going to play somewhere else, she wanted to connect with a different school as soon as possible and he called his longtime friend Dr. Forrest Pascal and told him that Crissa is looking for a different school.

Dr. Forrest Pascal responded back to him about a school who is looking for a point guard in Arizona. He told her of the good news that he got from Dr. Pascal, and she decided that she would fly out and take a look at the school. So, she took the trip and went to the school and talked with the coach.

After talking with the coach, she fell in love with the ideal that she would have the opportunity to take this team to the play off. When she return home, they started the procedures to move to the state of Arizona.

This was a very emotional time in Crissa's life, she had to leave all of her relationships behind that she had built over the years. The hardest part was to leave her siblings and her mother, but for the love of the game, she knew in her heart she was never leaving them, but she was fulfilling her dream and vision no matter where it took her.

She knew that there was only one thing that was not being left behind, and that was daddy. "Daddy's love would go with her physically, love has no limits." She was right; daddy was not letting her go by herself.

Within two months, daddy and his little girl started the new journey to a new school that was rolling out the red carpet of making Crissa not only the leader of their varsity girls' basketball team but the energy of love helping the team.

When they arrived, love was all over the place, everyone was showing her love, and they even helped her dad to get a job because he moved there with her. Again, she was experiencing the love that she was always accustomed to, they had her to stay over several of the girls' homes that were on the team.

She made new friends forever, and that by itself was worth the trip. She was learning at first-hand how to lead and take a basketball team to the final championship game, and that's was worth the transition to Arizona.

Even though she helped them to go to the finals with the hope to win the championship and lost, still they came out winners anyhow because Crissa took the Mountain Ridge girl basketball team by the love of God to their final frontier, the state champions playoff.

Just before she graduated, Dr. Forrest Pascal again reached out to them by telling her daddy of an organization named IMG Academy. He told him that the great tennis players, Venus and Serena Williams, known as the Williams sisters, went to this academy.

So dad talked to Crissa about the ideal of her going to this academy instead of going to college, and she thought that was the best ideal ever. So, he called IMG to get all the information to enroll her into this academy, and they told him that he would first have to send a DVD tape of her, they wanted to see her skill level.

So, daddy asked them, what does that mean? IMG replied, the tape would tell them whether or not they would accept her into their program. So, Dr. Pascal and daddy picked out the best tape they could find to display her skill and talent as a basketball player.

They sent it to the academy, and they replied that they would accept her in the program and all they had to do was send them all the paper work and the cost for her to attend for one year. So now she was again ready to start a new journey to the state of Florida at the IMG Academy.

This would be greatest move for Crissa, she would be exposed to professional basketball players who trained during their off season to better their game. So, they left Arizona and went back to Pennsylvania to get her ready for her next journey.

He wanted her to experience another season of God's love for all the hard work she had done and the love that she always shared with others who likes basketball. Her mother and father were very excited and thankful before God.

So, her mother and father drove her all the way to Florida to her new adventure of love and basketball. While she was there, she did a lot of training and playing basketball games with other girls who were going to the IMG Academy.

As a student of the sport called basketball, Crissa, during her time there gave them one hundred percent, and before you know it, she was all done with IMG. There was a college university who needed a point guard, and Crissa was recommended by IMG.

The name of the school was Savannah State University and someone that worked on staff was connected with the staff at Savannah Basketball Department, and they accepted her and gave her a four-year free ride.

So, she started to prepare herself for her next journey to play college basketball, which was big-time ball, and she was more excited than she has ever been in her life. She have been ready to live on her own, make her own decisions, and start living her life around the atmosphere and community of basketball.

As the point guard of the team, she became one of the leaders of the team, and her stats were more outstanding than most of the players on her team. Daddy flew in Savannah and rented a kitchenette for almost a month and a car to take a closer look at the life of a female basketball player in college which was his daughter.

He also wanted to see how strong her game was after going to IMG Academy, he was the only person in her life to train her since she was six years old, and he knew he would be able to see and tell how better she has become since she went to the IMG Academy.

He was very happy for her because the next step of her life was professional basketball, and he watched her develop into a professional star player who believed in herself all these years that she would become a star that gives light and love to all of those males or females who like to handle that basketball.

Up until this point, he had not talked about anything that was negative and the time has come where she must know the truth and the truth will set her free. She always had negative opposition since she was a little baby girl.

The enemy which is the devil has always attacked her in so many ways, especially the older she became and the better she became in basketball. But as long as her mother and daddy were with her, the enemy was always retreating because of the love of God.

No one is free of being attack, lie on, talked about, deceived, drugs, sexual immorality, and many other things that describe how sin abound, he always helped her to understand that God's grace is much more abounding through her love for the game of basketball.

The good news is where sin abounds, the love of God will abound much more than you will ever understand, it will always be your responsibility to provide the love of basketball to further your career and to endure the love journey.

In other words, the love of God restrains you, it keeps you from responding negatively. It's one of the only spiritual forces that are able to constrain you while you are trying to make a career out of the sport of your choice.

If you want to know more about the love of God, then the author would encourage you to get his new book called "The Royal Love Law" that would enlighten your flight to help your son or daughter to become one of the greatest sport players of all time.

You must always remember that the light and love that she brings to basketball is true love for the game, which is from God, and the devil is always trying to put her light out and cut off her ability to share the love of Jesus through compassion, emotion, and feelings, which is one of the ways that people are drawn to God.

Have you ever heard that God draws people through loving kindness? Loving kindness has always been one of the spiritual mysteries of how people are brought into a loving relationship with God and each other.

After being back home in San Diego, California for two years, dad got a call from Crissa from Savannah State University that she wanted to come to California to go to school, so he called his dear friend Dr. Forrest Pascal, and he began to research the area and found a school in the San Diego area called Point Loma University.

Dr. Pascal called him and told him that he talked to the coach of the girls' basketball team, and the coach said that he could use a good point guard. Dad contacted Crissa and told her all the information that was given to him by Dr. Forrest Pascal.

She immediately contacted the coach and began to make the preparation for transition to a San Diego, Californian school called Point Loma University. Daddy has entered into her life again to finish doing the things he always loved to do and that was going to her games.

Did you know that the love of God will never leave you or forsake you? When you trust that God is trying to love you at all times on your journey, God wants you to be able to use his love so you can have him with you at all times.

There are going to be times when you are seeking to follow your heart to do something in your life that need God' love to overcome. Again, Crissa was able to make transition to go to the girls' basketball program at Point Loma University for free for her last two years of basketball as a business major.

Daddy's little girl was becoming a smart and intelligent basketball stateswomen player. Somehow, she knew that the school Savannah State could not further her career, so she for many reasons relocated and moved to San Diego, California to do her last two years at Point Loma University.

She was a smart young woman who knew when it was time to move forward in love to better the opportunity for her future or what some people might say her destiny. This was a great time for dad because it brought to his attention how the love of God brought them back together once again after being separated for over three years.

At this time, dad was living in San Diego, and he was happy because he could go to all of her games and enjoy watching her living the dream. It was again another fun time for Crissa and daddy to spend time together; having cook outs and sleeps overs at each other's homes.

Daddy actually traveled all over California to watch every game she played and drove her home after the games when it was allowed. Point Loma was actually on top of mountain overlooking all of the county of San Diego and the ocean.

Standing on the mountain top of Point Loma was the most beautiful sights over the ocean and view of down town city of San Diego, this is a city you will want to see sometime in your travel from the mountain top. Dad loved it when she would have home games because he would always gaze over the ocean and the beautiful city of San Diego, which is a sight to view.

For two years, he watched and observed how she would lead her team to one victory after another, having so much fun, playing one game after another. Her stats were high in shots, in steals, and in assists.

She was always being interview and named as the most valuable player. Because she was born in the San Diego County at the Grossmont Hospital, dad could see that she was happy because she could finish her education in the same state and county where she was born and raised.

California will always be the state where she was birth into the Love of Basketball. This truly is the time where she received the call and gift to play and train in basketball from the age of six years old on the streets of El Cajon, California.

Now when she looks out from the state of California and discovered that her current coach was connected to Overseas Women Professional Basketball. She did accept the fact that she was not going to be drafted or try out for the WNBA.

That didn't stop her because she was not draft to the WNBA, she decided not to try out and decided to take a shot at Oversees Woman Professional Basketball, she talked to her coach about Overseas Women Professional Basketball and the coach connected her and she was thrilled, she knew of many players who would go overseas and play for a couple of years before they played for WNBA.

So, she told daddy about her plan to play Overseas Women Professional Basketball in the country of Germany. He was so excited when she told him of the good news. That's when he asked her, when are you planning to go?

She said, she was going to contact the organization in Germany and prepare her travel arrangements. So, she flew to Germany on another assignment and journey, to play and live as a "Women Professional Basketball Player."

She returned and told me, she made one of the basketball teams there, and they picked her to play on their team. Later they got back to her concerning the finance after they had offered her full-time pay, to call her later and to tell her that the owner changed her full-time salary to half of the money, leaving her to have to get a part-time job to pay for her overhead.

Crissa, with business sense, knew that she would have to be able to eat, and she said that she was not going to put herself in that position. She worked too hard not to get the right opportunity to play "Women Professional Basketball," especially being in another country with no family or help.

So, while she was waiting for her opportunity, she decided to start her own business, she had a BA Business degree. She specialized in body-building training, and she was very successful by receiving her certification to be able to train others.

She was not quitting basketball; she was training people in body building and basketball whenever she had the opportunity. Then she decided to move back to Harrisburg PA where all her family lived. She had ideals that she wanted to start building in Pennsylvania.

Her dad was visiting his family when Crissa moved back and he was invited to his nephew (Alfred Jackson) wedding. When he arrived, he saw Crissa old friend Chris Franklin and began to talk to him about Crissa just moving back to Harrisburg PA.

Mr. Chris Franklin, known as Mr. Handles from the Nikki team, told him that he was a Harlem Globe Trotter now and he wanted to talk to Crissa, so daddy gave Mr. Franklin her number. Now you have to understand that his daughter used to travel with Chris Franklin (Niki Trick Team) for years.

His daughter left Pennsylvania at the age of sixteen to go to Arizona, and Mr. Chris Franklin left the Niki Trick Team and became a Harlem Globe Trotter. Mr Chris Franklin was in the best position to help her by telling her that there will be a tryout for women to play on the team.

Mr. Chris Franklin was always her mentor and did what a mentor would do to help. Crissa put together a tape that had to be prepared for the Harlem Globe Trotter to look at and accept before she could become a candidate for tryout.

She was accepted to tryout and began to practice her routine over and over again. Finally, she went to the tryout and blew them away. What was different about her trying out was, no one ever spins a ball on one finger with both hands at the same time.

When she gave them her tape, she spinned two balls, one on each hand to one finger at the same time, and dad knew that they have never saw any female do that before at that level of competition. She took a ball in her left and a ball in her right hand and spun both of them on each finger at the same time.

It was incredible, she performed all of the other tricks that the Harlem Globe Trotter did during their show. All this was recorded on tape, and dad knew that she was going to blow them away during the tryouts.

It was not very long that they got back to her and told her that she made the Harlem Globe Trotter Team, and she became one of the happiest women in the world. During her first two years, she had travel all over the world.

She blessed her family to be able to go and see her perform at her shows. She is one of the greatest entertainers of all time with that ball in her hands, and all the children and kids loved her because she became that child in heart, when she was showing them the love of basketball from her heart of her soul.

She has always been able to connect with love when it came to basketball, because she has always had that inner connection with the art and skill of the love of basketball. Daddy's little girl was truly blessed by God to understand how to love the game of basketball from the very beginning of her childhood even until today.

Notice he said, she was blessed to understand God's love at an early age, and this would be an important factor for any parent to prepare themselves to teach and train their children in the love of God as early as possible.

Her love for basketball opened up one of the greatest opportunities for her to be able to let the world see her passion and compassion for the game. You have to watch her love in action, God will enable you to see with your heart how she cares for the ones who want to learn the love of the game called basketball.

Every move and turn that she does when she is handling the ball is her way of expressing her love to the game of basketball to the world. This is just the beginning of her learning how to show her love to the whole wide world to be able to see that she is the love gift to the game called basketball.

The world will see that this girl is on fire, and when she handles the ball, it always give the allusion that the ball is moving with flames of fire. Her fans have not seen all that she can do with that ball and have not heard about all the places that she will be performing in the future because of her love for basketball.

You definitely have not heard the last of the basketball legend called Crissa Jackson the ball handler. All things will work together for the good in the future because her performance will grow in the love of the game for others to participate.

If you are following daddy train of thought, you will see and witness that her destiny with the Harlem Globe Trotter was just a stepping stone so she could move on to bigger and better opportunities that awaits her through social media.

Take this to the bank of your heart; she did not join the Harlem Globe Trotters for the money. If so, she would not have joined the Harlem Globe Trotters, her dad thinks they only pay their new players a little over twenty thousand a year to start with their company. For Crissa, she was in love with basketball and not the money.

With Crissa, it was never about the money or the honey, it was always about the opportunity to show love and entertain the people. Basketball taught Crissa that the love of the game has its own way of revealing to you who you really are as a sport player.

She has always been a game-changer for the benefit of the people, and because of her true love for the game, she will always be able to show love to every boy and girl basketball lover. She will

give all them a glance of the love from her heart for the game called basketball.

Her love in action will always be remembered by all the boys and girls all over the world. God so loved the world that he gave you Crissa Jackson, a young female who sacrificed all of her life for the love of the game of basketball.

If you are an agent or salesman for a major company that is looking for a female basketball player who can do magic with the ball by spinning one ball with one hand and spin the other on the other hand at the same time is a winning combination.

He hopes that the love of God gives you the revelation through reading this book concerning the love sacrifice that Crissa gave for the love of the game. So, dreams, visions, and hopes will be fulfilled in the hearts of millions of boys and girls all around the world.

This should be one of those moments where you are feeling the call to sacrifice yourself for the love of the game like you have never known to do before in your life for anything. This is who you are now and who you will become, "A Game Changer"

THE LOVE PERSONALITY

If you want to know about Crissa Jackson's personality, her dad can give you some information, but the rest, you are going to have to meet up with her while she is journeying near a state where you live. Crissa, is dad's most important and best writing ever, he is writing about how she develop her personality.

The word personality means, her set of behaviors on the outside, and the word characteristics means her moral behaviors on the inside. The totality of her attitudes, interests, behavioral patterns, emotional responses, social roles, and other individual traits that endure over long periods of time is what this chapter is all about, when it talks about Crissa Jackson as the love personality.

One of the most distinctive parts of her personality and character is her being very noticeable, which makes her socially appealing, a famous person, especially an entertainer or athlete. Daddy's little girl who was delivered from her mother's womb was first the love gift from God to her parents to show her love before her conception.

The person daddy is talking about is a female who was delivered on October 26, 1989 with long straight black hair covering her face with black eye brows and pretty brown skin with beautiful eyes, ears, and nose at the time of birth.

She was very beautiful, lovely, attractive, gorgeous and stunning as a little baby; she looked more like a Mexican baby called a bambina. Her first outfit was a red baby outfit that mommy and daddy picked out in Mexico before she was born.

She had the appearance of a Mexican baby with more of the Indian from daddy's side of the family. She was a good baby even at birth as she lay there, peaceful and restful. Crissa was able to sleep alone listening to the soft and precious music that her mother always prepared and played for her until it cut off or she falls asleep.

Her mother was able to get some rest because of Crissa good nature, and she drank breast milk that was pumped during the day and frozen and warmed up by her daddy at night and fed to her by her daddy. Crissa was a breast-fed baby and daddy believed that was one of the reason that caused her to have closeness and love with her mother.

All of her life, she has had a serious attitude which showed everyone a personal view of her feelings about people she didn't know, a positive attitude to change once she gets to know you. Crissa outward bodily posture and language, shows her friends, family the person she is growing up to be, especially in sports.

When you engaged in a conversation with her, you would discern that she is sport wise with an attitude to challenge and be assertive in the conversation. All of her life, she has been a person of interests, she has feelings of curiosity and concern about things that turns her attention towards her relationships with her family and basketball.

She also has love power for success that draws people to her wherever she travels in the world, she is always enjoying something or someone, she loves training, bodybuilding, and working with kids at an early age.

She has always had interest in benefiting or being able to take advantage of life opportunities, her involvements allowed her to make progress or success with people. As far back as daddy can remember, her behavioral patterns were that of good conduct, her ability to manage and control others, and her personal life was always intact.

She always loves to perform in sports, expressing her skill level in basketball. She is a person of action, energetic activities, working towards her goal; she always doing something in order to achieve her purpose in life.

She is very goal-orientated and would let nothing get in her way from the goals that needed to get done. She was also a person that is used to getting things done, from as far back as her daddy could remember.

She is a person who does a lot of activities like energetic physical movement or exercise, being active every day as far back as he could remember. She is connected to all the people that follow her through social media.

She always used the same manner of personality in her life as a pattern throughout her childhood to young adult hood. She has become emotionally responsive to everyone and anyone regarding behavior patterns.

She would relate to or express her emotion to others, she is very easy going by nature, easily affected by or patience to express her emotion and feeling to certain individual, especially after she gets to know you better.

She has been characterized by her emotion, especially when it comes to the love of basketball, inspired by those emotions cause her to have insight and will power towards her visions and dreams.

She has a strong passion, feeling, and excitement for success in the game of basketball from the age of six until the presence. She is a person of fire, full of enthusiasms, delight, thrill, and eagerness to learn and became a better student of the love of the game called basketball.

She trained and practice by herself for many years which help to build and create the personality that she is working with today. Her personality throughout social media is helping her to build her followers that keep growing.

You have to understand that she did not have the time to build normal social relationships growing up as a kid. She might only have two real friends until she got to middle school. Because of basketball, she became one of the most popular girls in her schools for the remaining of her educational and basketball life.

She became good when relating to society in the way which people in groups behave and interact. She was growing and maturing in meetings and interacting with friends, family, and Christians. Because of her Christian background, she was able to relate to the human welfare of people from all walks of life and those who were not Christian.

Growing up as a little girl, she played with dolls babies but not that much, what she really liked was her hamster that she would play with almost every day. She did not like to share very much with others unless they were very close to her.

She loved to go swimming in the pool at an early age with floaters. She really loved the water more and more as she got older. One of her favorite play times was riding her bike, and the older she got, the more she liked to ride her bike throughout the city.

She was a young hustler with three means to make money, one was walking dogs, two was cleaning elderly neighbor's houses, and third, she would buy discount candy and sell it at school and in the neighborhood.

At a young age, she would develop a business and decide to go on and major in business in college and graduated with a bachelor degree in business. She would always act like a jokester, trying to be funny and at the same time trying to humor you.

She is a lot of fun to be around, she is a happy person, she is very compassionate to everyone and could make friends very easy. She knows how to hold onto her friends and when it comes to her parents, she is very respectful all the time.

She would never raise her voice or say something smart to them. She always conducted herself as a very well-mannered child. Now, try to understand, she did have another side to her that helps her to be balanced in life.

She was not always a goodie two-shoes, in other words, she was not better than anyone else when it came to bad attitude. Starting early in life when her brother (Jay) or sisters (Aleena and Marilyn) would try to take anything from her, she would have a fit. She would tell them what's on her mind with a bad attitude.

Her bad attitude turned into a calm attitude, where she will now tell you calmly not to treat or talk to her any kind of way. She learned to keep herself with a disposition that would limit anyone to approach her in a negative way.

That gave her some control over how she would maintain her love personality and not hate. During her discipline years, she only received the rod (according to the bible, when you spare the rod, you spoil the child) maybe five times in her whole life, and her mommy did that, not her daddy, she could not handle the thought of him putting the rod on her butt.

She would start crying before her mother would hit her on her butt. She was very sensitive when it came to getting discipline with the rod and that maybe once a year. Sometimes she was very selfish about sharing with others, because she was the baby, she always told her mother that something or someone was doing to her.

She was her mother's baby, being protected against the older kids. Most of the time, she would not share with anyone the things that meant so much to her, she treasured everything she would get and take good care of it by not sharing it with anyone.

When she started playing basketball, her personality and character started to change based on her hard work of practice and training with the love of God. Basketball began to develop her love personality, she poured everything that was in her heart to develop her skills and techniques.

But at the same time, he could see that the love of basketball was shaping, influencing, modeling, molding, sculpting, and forming her love personality to be that star that she saw in her destiny. She was very educated during the years of elementary, middle school, and high school.

She was an honorary student all through school, and she hated school with a passion, she felt that it was taking time from her love training and practicing. She would get help always from other girls or boys during her school experience.

She would tell him about the kids at school, how they would help her with her homework and her test. She said, because of her popularity, she would ask them always for their help, and they would not turn her down.

One thing that she knew is this, if she did not keep up her grades, she would not be able to play basketball, and that forced her to guarantee herself that she was going to play basketball and no education was going to stop that.

She also was very competitive when it comes to having a high-grade point average, she work very hard to be the "A" student before the eyes of her sisters and brother. She was an honorary student that works hard to be recognize every year.

Because of her popularity at school and other places, she wanted to be recognized as a smart basketball player and not a stupid sport player. Thank God, she was able to carry this view and discipline all the way through college, capitalizing on every student's ability to help her get through the educational part of her life.

You must remember that she did not like school from the very start of kindergarten, and during her practice and training throughout the years, all she did was complain about homework and tests. Daddy knew that all he had to do is remind her about this one thing all the time.

It was other schools' athletic departments who were always checking on her grades to find a way for her not to play basketball. The sport of basketball had a lot to do with Crissa becoming the love personality, who she is today.

Love and basketball will continue to shape her love personality until she reaches her destiny. You will have to trust the process of the love of the Holy Spirit, who guided and comfort her continually as she worked hard for her money.

The bible says, in First Corinthians chapters twelve and thirteen, "now I will show you the most excellent way, if you speak in the tongues of men and of angels, but have not love, you are only a resounding gong or a clanging cymbal."

In other words, if Crissa would not have put love into her basketball practice and training, she would only have gone through the motions with no sense of feel. Because of love, her basketball skills continue to develop her love personality.

All daddy is saying, you got to give your heart to the game, put your emotions and your feelings into the practice and training every time you step on the track and the court. This is what you will have to work on every time you practice and train.

If you don't, you will never be able to let love help you to grow in the sport. If you have the gift of prophecy and can fathom all mysteries and all knowledge, and if you have faith that can move mountains and have not love, you are nothing in the sports world.

In other words, if you don't operate by faith through love, you will not be able to become a sport star. In other words, you got to believe in what you're doing in sports, and you got to put love into play when you are training and practicing.

Always be reminded that you've got to put these two into your workouts every time to practice or train. Faith plus love equals greatness! If you don't, you will never grow, but you will discover that love believes and hopes in all things, he is talking about your basketball practice and training.

You would end up becoming nothing with the sport of your choice and will not end of successful in your final destiny. If you give all your money to the poor and surrender your body to the flames, but have not love, you will gain nothing.

In other words, if you pour your body, mind, and spirit into basketball training and practicing, a sport of your choice without the love of God, you will not be able to profit, gain or benefit, your "reward" at the end of your destiny in the sport of your choice is "failure."

Can you spiritually see how God is developing her love personality and character to be a winner and not a loser, a finisher and not a quitter, through his love for basketball? Love is patient, which is a character builder, and she knew that it would take time for her to develop her love personality through her character.

Love is kind, which is another character builder, and she knew that she had to learn to treat people who are involved in her circle of basketball with love. Love does not envy, which is another character builder, and she knew that she would have to grow in that area to not be jealous of others success.

Crissa does not focus of somebody else success, but focus and work hard towards her own personal mission to succeed in the love for basketball. Love is not proud, which is another character builder and she knew that she had to prepare herself so that she did not get lifted up in pride, because pride comes just before destruction and a haughty spirit just before a fall.

She knows that she has to stay humble and lowly in the spirit of her character in order to overcome pride, which is love at its best through personality. Love is not rude, bad-mannered, impolite, offensive, and foul-mouth, which is another character builder.

Crissa knows that the power of the tongue is able to speak life or death, but she has chosen to speak words of positivity, helpful, encouraging which shares love and life to everyone. She speaks words of creativity, original, imaginative, inspired, inventive, resourceful, ingenious, and productive, so she can create a positive picture of her love personality and destiny.

Listen carefully, my reader, because love is not easily angered, annoyed, irritated, frustrated, or provoked, which is another character builder, and she is constantly working to develop her personality, especially that anger she had as a little girl as far as he can remember.

She knows that she cannot have anger controlling her life, especially when she becomes a role model. She learned early that temperance is love under control, in other words, love is helping her to control her anger, and she has become that love personality who works hard to control of her anger.

One of life's best kept secrets, is for you to forgive, if you don't forgive, you'll have lock yourself in your own cage for life. It is a God-given fact that you will stunt your growth. Remember, God made it this way so you will forgive like he has forgiven you seven-times-seventy.

Remember, if you forgive, love keeps no records, archives, accounts, histories, files, or reports of wrong doing, which is another character builder, she has been working hard on her personality from a child, not to store up in her heart how people have done wrong to her down through the years.

She is fully aware that God's love is keeping her from digging up all the wrong that has been done to her. She learned early in life, she needed to forgive as she has been forgiven. This is very important if you want to move forward in your dream and vision.

She learned to cast all her cares on Jesus, he truly cares for her, and that is what she has worked hard to do for her love personality to grow as a person. Love does not delight, have pleasure, seek happiness or amusement in evil but rejoices, celebrates, expresses joy and is glad when it hears the truth.

This is another truth that is a character builder, and she tried very hard to be above approach, but at the end of the day if she falls, she gives it all to God in Christ Jesus. One important point, you need to know about Crissa, like most, she grew up in a dispensation where kids made God and Christ Jesus personal in their heart.

Her relationship with God was truly intense and personal and she will not discuss it with anyone she didn't know. But when it comes to show time with the basketball, she has a way to let her light shine in the darkest areas during a performance. She has that gift of love that produces good ball handling.

When she puts the two together, the love and basketball, she transforms into God's love personality. Loves always protects, defends, guards, keeps, shields, and shelters her from seen and unseen danger. She stands out like a love light on a hill that can't be hid.

Love always hopes, always trusts, and always perseveres, these virtues are character builders for her personality, she has known faith through love since she was a little girl, and now it is her season to prosper and capitalize from all of her hard work.

She has grown in every area, and when you look at her love profile, you will be able to witness what God has done for her through her love personality. When she was a child, she thought, acted, talked, and walked like a child.

After Crissa started applying the love of God in her life, she began to grow and started putting away negative behavior. Because of hard work ethics, she has been able to mature in her love personality, this is the Holy Spirit working through her personality.

Because of God's love, she has been able to fully know the will of God for her destiny in basketball to become a star. She has discovered that it is very important to have hoped, confidence, expectation, courage, and to have faith, belief, and assurance of love.

Here is what stands out the most about her, is the fact that God's love is greater than any love that she has ever experienced. Daddy wants you to understand that all that she has become is because she dared to love when she was very young.

All he's saying to you, it doesn't take knowledge, understanding, or wisdom to get this love from God. All you have to do is open up your heart and ask God to give you one of his most precious gifts, and he will deposit that gift into your heart if you repent and except Jesus.

God's love put Crissa in the best positive position, it developed her foundation so she could have her love personality grow to be the person to show that love to all people that God puts in her world of basketball and business.

While she was growing, she knew in her heart that God's love was going to give her the best love personality that she needed in order to become successful in her life. In other words, any female that gives their heart to Jesus will take on a new love personality.

If any woman (Crissa) is in Christ, she is a new creature, old nature is passing away and a new nature is given to her. In other words, she took on God's new love nature believing that God is love. What that supposed to mean to you, her new nature is God's love personality.

That love has allowed her to be prune by the Holy Spirit down through the years to be nurture, cultivate, foster, develop, raise, and rear up throughout the years to become a love personality for the twenty-first-century.

The point to be taken here is, there is only one true method and process that is positive to help any child to have a very good mental, positive love personality while growing up. He thanked God for his little girl who trusted the Holy Spirit to develop in her "The Love Personality."

CHAPTER NINE

THE LOVE
CHARACTER

B efore he shares with you the character of Crissa since she's was a little girl, he would like for you to take a look at the word character from two definitions which he thinks will help you to see her more in the character than ever before.

The first definitions, taken from Merriam Webster, a person who says or does funny or unusual things for an example, your friend is quite a character. A person who is distinguished by some unusual quality held in particular esteem, and always distinguished from others of the same category, one that is used for a special service or occasion.

The second definition, from got Questions.org where character is defined as strength of moral fiber. A.W. Tozer described character as "the excellence of moral beings." As the excellence of gold is its purity and the excellence of art is its beauty, so the excellence of a woman is her character.

Persons of character are noted for their honesty, ethics, and charity (love in action). Descriptions such as "woman of principle and woman of integrity" are assertions of character. According to Thesaurus: English (U.S English.), assertion means affirmations and affirmation means encouragement by way of support.

A lack of character is moral deficiency, and persons lacking character tend to behave dishonestly, unethically, and uncharitably. A woman's character is the sum of her disposition, thoughts, intentions, desires, and actions.

In other words, according to the context of this book, a love character is what daddy's little girl is blessed to develop through her relationship with God the Holy Spirit, to achieved and accomplished the things inside her heart concerning the love of basketball.

You have heard the vernacular (according to Encarta Dictionary, vernacular means the everyday language of the people in a country or region; the common spoken language of a people) saying that she's a character.

Daddy has always said, Crissa is a character ever since she was a little girl. She would dress up all the time and walk around the house like she was a little lady. She would let her siblings put make-up on her and dress her up just so she could humor the family.

She was quite a character and still is quite a character. It was always the expressions on her face that would either make you laugh or just say that she's a character and a half. As she got older, she would dance like her siblings or as some may say, she would copy their dance as a way to entertain her family.

Her character was the definition of someone who says or does funny or unusual things to show love. As she got older, she would start dancing and singing like Michael Jackson. She would love to entertain her family.

She was always making funny faces and talking funny to make you laugh. Her character just got bigger, during middle school up to high school and even in college, she created her owned signature dance.

She tries to be funny by always imitating the Michael Jackson moon walk just like her brother. She was known by her school friends and basketball players (even while playing with the Harlem Globetrotter) to break out during a game, practice, and after a game by doing the Michael Jackson moon walk.

Whenever the family gets together on holidays or special occasions, the little girl down in side of her who loves to express herself in many different ways would do something to humor everyone. There was another character inside of her that has been nurture by her mom and dad since she was a baby.

This is Crissa character of love, a character that is the foundation of who she really is as a person. Her mother and father made sure that God deposited through the years virtues of love down in her heart. Her heart is full of love that embodies not only her emotions, but also her mental strength and physical love for the game of basketball.

God told her when she was young to love. Like many of you, God said, "Love the Lord thy God with all thy heart." He is saying that she had to give all of her inner being, outer being, whether physical, mental, or spiritual, to him.

Daddy thanked God for his love, he gave himself completely and totally in life service of worship and praise through basketball training. These are the spiritual heart qualities that apply to you and daddy's little girl. These are just some of the things that you are going to have to work on, in order to establish the love character.

Crissa was taught to have a willing heart that will help her character to be strong and loving on the track and gym. She was taught to cooperative in order to become a good-hearted person when training. Crissa's love character has given her the ability to establish a wise heart that is able to make sensible decisions and judgments while on or off the track and court.

Also, she was trained to show good sense and judgment that is based on the knowledge about taking care of her business on and off the track and basketball court. This meant everything to Crissa to be able to demonstrate the love of the game through a loving character.

Lastly, because of the love character of God, she is very capable of achieving her purpose or goal by showing skill, shrewdness, and ingenuity. When it comes to planning or doing something that will bring forth much fruit (love in action) in her relationship with God and basketball, she has built good working ethics on or off the track and the basketball court.

She was taught by her daddy to have an understanding heart, to be able to accept the things that she could not change or control, especially on or off the track and basketball court. An understanding heart gave her the ability to perceive and explain the meaning or the nature of somebody or something to the girls she would be instructing on or off the track and basketball court.

Crissa would always try to help her girlfriends to understand all that she was doing and how that would help their basketball skills. She was taught in the education system to try to understand what others are trying to make sense of when it comes to sport.

Crissa is always ready to take care of her business on and off the track or basketball court. She was train to have a caring heart that would show compassion or concern for others people's physical, spiritual or their general welfare.

She has the kind of love character that would try to make provision for food, clothing, or other types of care, either professionally or in general for family and friends that are less fortunate. She was taught gentleness, which is one of the virtues of the Fruit of the Spirit, which is connected to the love character that comes from God.

By training her in the Fruit of Love, she has been able throughout her career to handle all of her business relationships with calmness. She was taught how to have a serving heart to be able to serve people who want to learn about basketball.

He is talking about talk shows, TV advertisement, social media, and doing live basketball shows. Please understand, she understood that it is very important to love the game of basketball. Crissa is the person who learned as much as she could about God's love's character, it is one of the keys to her success spiritually and physically on social media.

She tried to listen very closely to her heart, especially when the Holy Spirit is trying to speak to her, she knew how to adjust to her development of her love character. She continued to grow in every area of God's love. She knew that the process of love would eventually help her morality.

So, her daddy began to teach more and more about the love of God, she was maturing in discerning between good and bad, happy and sad in the hearts of people and in the world of basketball. Especially, when playing in a game or traveling around the world.

She would discover her ability to use her spiritual senses through her love for the game, and she was able to discern offense and defense being the point guard during the game. Daddy began to teach her about the sowing and reaping principle concerning her love character, how the seed of love will be planted in her heart to produce a strong character.

In other words, he was just hoping and praying that the sowing and planting through teaching of love would travel down into her heart, causing the love of God to give birth, shape, and destiny to her character.

Her daddy would explain to her that she is new to learning how to love the game of basketball. She was told if you want to mature in the love of game, you have to practice five days a week. When you mature in your love for the game, you will apply your love to your training and practicing.

You will also gain experience and produce the skills like discerning the offense and defense by making game plays. She was starting to learn and understand that love is the product that produces positive results from your heart to the sport.

Her experience down through the years has taught and shown her that love is the fruit of the spirit, which is the very love nature and character of God inside of her spiritual heart and not the physical heart.

You see, she was not born with spiritual character, she was nurture by the spirit of love from birth as she was growing. As one man stated, "If she takes care of her character, her reputation will take care of itself." In other words, building a strong character will protect your reputation in sports and her personal life.

Another man once said, "If she creates a character, she creates a destiny." Because she has developed great character, daddy searched books and the internet, to discover a truth about character, that the word character is developed, shaped, and formed from the word love, which is God in Christ Jesus.

The definition for character can only be found through the study of etymology from the English interpretation, which means a set of qualities that make somebody or something distinctive, especially somebody's qualities of mind and feeling, strength of mind, resolution, independence, individuality, moral quality, position, rank, or capacity.

The reason why daddy is sharing this information with you is because there is no other way for him to be able to describe her character the way that it is defined and explain in some of these definitions comparing to God's love.

This type of love character you are not born with, you have to accept Jesus into your heart by repenting, and she accepted him when she was very young. She accepted Jesus through confessing and believing in her heart that Jesus died for her sins because he loved her.

According to her faith, the scriptures said in the book of 2 Corinthians 5:17, any woman in Christ is a new creature, old things pass away, and all things become new. The understanding here is to inform you, so you can understand her process and the transition that took place when she was a child.

God deposited into her the love character that was going to help her to make the journey to her destiny. This is the understanding that you need to know, his little girl received a new spiritual love nature, which means the old patterns of behavior was transformed to a new nature, which is now her new love character inside of her.

Ever since this transformation, she has been committed, dedicated, loyal, faithful with temperance (self-control), and able to continue on her journey for the love of basketball, even until today through social media into the years to come.

The love of God has developed her character over the years, she can now do the things that she has worked so hard for all of her life. She is ready to take love where ever she goes in this world. It was so important that she build a strong character through love from her youth into the years to come.

Have you ever met a love child like daddy's little girl? Well wait until you get a hold of her, she has a whole lot of character that will make you fall in love with her at first site. Remember on the outside she attracts and draws you to her personality, but it is the strong character inside of her heart that would inspire you for greatness.

She has been so blessed to work hard on the inside (character) and outside (personality) to be able to mature in personality and character. She has defined who she is by developing a beautiful spiritual loving magnet that draws people to her love for the game.

One of the reasons why she has been blessed by God's love in her heart, is to be able to draw as many people as she can through the power of love. For one to understand how the power of love draws people to God, must understand the love of God.

Sharing her heart filled with the love character has been one of things she used throughout her training and practicing, it gave her a winning relationship with everyone all over the world. There is power in having a strong character of love.

Her love has never fail her; her love will endure all things, hope in all things, and believe in all things. Her love will constraint her whenever she is in a negative situation. Her love will give her the power to love all people no matter what is the color of their skin or the walk of life they come from.

Her faith will express her belief through love, and her heart will follow the path of that same love. She has grown to be an extraordinary, magnificent, wonderful, loving woman with a strong character, theoretically speaking, "first place runner or second to none."

All of this has happened to her over a period of 25 years, she dared to let God change her nature from the natural character to the spiritual love character, so she can be a star full of love. She is the one that will able to spread her love throughout the social media.

SECTION THREE

CRISSA
THE FIRE BALL
PART 3
TRUE LOVE ONLY

CHAPTER TEN

THE SPORT EVANGELIST

He wants the reader to know that this chapter is all about his belief and hope that one day a sports evangelist will be born of God into the Jackson's family. His belief started a long time ago, it was heating up as the years were passing.

In this short chapter, he would like to talk about how he saw her not literal, at the beginning of her journey as a sport evangelist.

But as the years were passing, he literally watch her become the sport evangelist of the twenty first century.

He would like for you to travel with him in thought briefly, as he shares with you the inspiration in his mind and heart about the thoughts and ideals he was having about Crissa being called to be an international sport evangelist.

His thoughts of her reaching out to young people began when she got to middle school and when she traveled to the Amsterdam in the Netherlands and came back as the MVP; she was so excited to share her love for basketball.

There were all kind of ideals and thoughts about how he would love to see his little girl sharing the love of God as a sport evangelist in the twenty first century. Traveling all over the world sharing and helping people in the sport world.

Many parents live with thoughts throughout their life about how they would like their children to turn out in life, and he is given the privilege to write his down on paper in this book for the world to read. When you are given the God opportunity to raise a child up in the way they should go, in the back of your mind, you would be thinking, will this child follow my footsteps?

Would this child become the person that will have the same gift as he does and take it to the next level? He would always say to himself, "it would be nice to see daddy's little girl preaching all over the world." Sharing her basketball skills with love to the sports world would give God the opportunity to help every boy or girl to love the game through her.

It all started when he was a young married man who was called and commissioned to preach the gospel of our lord and savior Jesus Christ, and like most married men, they have to make a decision on how they are going to make choices of serving the gift.

He chose to do both, he felt his family was first to be evangelized. But back in his mind, he wanted to travel and build a life as a traveling evangelist. Knowing in his heart he had to make the right decision to evangelize his family.

He started to invest in his children, and when he discovered that he had a little girl who had a vision to play basketball as a professional, he found himself dedicated to the cause. In the back of his mind, he was always thinking, could she be the one that would carry on my gift or maybe it will be one of the other siblings?

It was hard to tell, he began to incorporate all of them slowly to do the work of the evangelist. First, he would have them to learn how to pass out flyers door to door, next to be involve in a dance ministry team that would allow them to travel throughout the San Diego county called "Kingdom Kids," lead by their mother who loves to dance and sing.

Then he began to focus by narrowing down to help his little girl to train as his little sports evangelist. She would do everything he asked her, no matter what it was; he knew she is so easy to train, so responsible and workable. He decided to take her by his side like the rest of the kids and share his gift.

When she becomes successful, she is going to have to make a choice or do both basketball and evangelize the gospel through the love of sports. So, the years were going bye, he kept his little girl close to God and himself, he kept on traveling around her known world to different churches and basketball camps so she would get both training from outside coaches and inside preachers rather than just her daddy.

In his mind, all he could see and hope for was his little girl to get a spiritual breakthrough for the love of the game and to be able to evangelize through love. He kept thinking, wouldn't that be a miraculous thing to happen for the Jackson's, if his little girl would go full time as a sports evangelist?

The bible says, that eyes have not seen and ears have not heard about the things that God has in stored for them that love him and is called for his purpose. Another scripture states, that all things will work together for her because of the love that she has for the game.

Every now and then, he would find himself in his mental world of figurative imagination that his little girl could turn out to be a sport evangelist. He would take her with him where ever he would go to church service, and she would know exactly what he was doing for the both of them.

Through reaching the lost souls and building a ball handle career, they were making things happen for the both of them. That has always been his way of sharing with her how building your sport career is a matter of how you are taking charge of the love of the game.

It is how the spiritual principle works in order for God to take care of sports business. He was beginning to think, meditate, and dream about her becoming a sport evangelist, and he knew he had to expose her to the things of the spirit that the Holy Spirit had shown him like soul winning, which is one of the keys to spiritual prosperity.

Sowing love, is another way for God to get to the heart of men and women, and he knew one day she would have that opportunity to sow love in the hearts of the people. His little girl ended up spending about twelve years together with him, just about every day from the age of six until eighteen, those years were incredible because most of the time it was intimate with great love being poured into the both of them.

He really knew that nothing could take the place of the love that they build together during those years. But always in the back of his mind, that belief was still occupying his heart that she might be the one to take the work of the evangelist to the next level, representing the gospel of our lord and savior Jesus Christ.

He always wanted to hear from others concerning their opinion about what they think when they see her perform as a professional basketball player. He always wanted to know whether or not that anyone could see the little evangelist in her waiting to come out to share the love of the game.

Remember, he is ordained, licensed as a writing and traveling evangelist, and called by the voice of God to evangelize for the rest of his life as a messenger of love. He trained her, and no one else has had the opportunity to train her in anything, for he was blessed of God to be the one and only trainer, teacher, pastor, and evangelist to have impact her life physically, mentally and spiritually.

Can somebody tell him where is his little sport evangelist and what is she is doing these days? She seems to be so busy that he can hardly keep up with her. Please somebody tell him when you see her,

"he is getting older now, and life is not as it was for him in his new discovery of kidney failure."

All he's hearing about is how she been traveling all over the world as a Harlem Globe Trotter. In the last few years she been playing basketball, causing children and family to smile and be full of laughter showing the world the love of a sport evangelist.

She has appeared on television a few times, and she has a strong following through social media by engaging them with the heart of a true sport evangelist. She will be able to draw more love from social media while sharing her love on her journey to the whole wide world.

CHAPTER ELEVEN

THE ENTERTAINER

Remember that good old song, the entertainer, she's an entertainer, the entertainer. As three years old, you could see the signs of an entertainer in her character, especially when she would try to entertain her siblings. She loved attention, and she would always get attention because she was the youngest of four children.

She loved laughing with her siblings while having a blast of fun all the time. One of the facts is that her siblings would get her to laugh especially her brother. The siblings used to dress her in different outfits and tell her to go show mom and dad.

She loved every moment of it because she was the center of attraction. There is something about being the center of attraction and all the attention is focus on you. Crissa loved all that attention that she would get from her family all the time.

What daddy used to tell his kids about the Jackson brothers, they used to entertain through dancing and singing all the time while growing up. They even dressed like they were entertainers and sometimes acted like they were entertainers.

He always looked for the showmanship that would flow through the blood line of all his kids. Mom or dad, just never knew who God might use to do what they always dreamed and thought in their minds and hearts.

Well, so far it was nothing but signs here and there that daddy and mommy would notice in her from time to time. Thinking that she is just being a kid having fun with the family to discover later when she got into gymnastics at the age of three, daddy could see the entertainer in her as long as somebody was watching her perform.

She loved the attention and the focus that was on her. It really became noticeable when she turned six years old and started to train and practice basketball. You would notice every now and then she would perform at the track. People used to tell her at the age of seven that she was going to be a good basketball player, and daddy really began to see the entertainer in her.

She would go on the basketball court to perform with skills that other kids did not have, and she would always get all the attention. She was usually the smallest girl but more skillful than the rest. It was becoming a constant thing with her, the harder she would train, her skill level got better, and it began to develop in her training.

When she would play in a game, people would always focus on her dribbling and shooting skills. Her training grounds and her court presence was becoming her stage for entertaining all those who were there watching. She was showing them what a little girl who trains hard could do with a basketball.

It was until she was in eighth grade that she went to her high school at that time, and there was a show by a team of men who were called Niki Trick Team. Now before she saw them perform, she used to play around and practice tricks so she could use them in her games.

She loved showing off during a basketball game by throwing the ball behind her back or crossing over or moving the ball around her back just before a shot. But that night at the high school, she saw those men do a number of tricks.

She immediately started trying to do them while she was watching. Daddy was watching her, to get her response after everything was over, and he had never seen her get so excited about tricks like he saw her at that show.

Daddy knew that the ball tricks that they were doing was something important and special to her, and so daddy found out where they were going to perform, and he made sure they attended there shows. Daddy noticed that she was practicing all of their routines, and it did not register that she was preparing herself for the show. You see, during the show, they would always pick out little kids to do tricks with them and helping them to do the tricks.

During one show, they picked out Crissa, and she actually did all of the tricks when they asked her. Daddy knew one of the showmen, he went to school with his nephew. Daddy told Mr. Chris Franklin that she loves what you do," and the showman saw that she was willing to learn and perform so they added her to their team.

She travels with them doing NBA intermission, and daddy saw the entertainer in her again. She loved to bow and sign autographs. She looked and acted like a star that she said she was going to be one day. Crissa was the happiest little girl in the world.

For the next several years, she would travel with the Niki Trick Team and play basketball for her school. The entertainer in her was developing every day, and she loved the life to the point that she started training her physical body to be strong enough to do the things that an entertainer must be able to do while entertaining her basketball audience.

Her true focus was to entertain her basketball fans and no one else. By the time she got to high school, she had established her stage and platform to entertain all who would come and see her play. Her fans would always give her the awe every time she would do some fancy move like the crossover, turnaround, or the three-point shot.

Her audience came expecting a show from her, and a show they would get. Her coach at Susquehanna High School would always tell her not to throw the ball behind her back and not to do anything fancy, just keep it simple.

But what they did not know was the show girl in her always wanted to come out of Crissa, in her mind eye, it was show time. It was in her to perform with that basketball any way she could perform to entertain her audience.

Most of her coaches could not see how gifted she was and that could of helped the team if they could have supported her for who she really was, truly she was the entertainer of the sport called love and basketball.

Her development by God was not just an incidence, God was making opportunity for her to be shaped, molded, and directed by the Holy Spirit through love every year of her life to be the greatest female entertainer of all times with that basketball.

He knew that if she could entertain people by making them happy and sending them home feeling better, whether you win or lose, they were entertained with a show of skill and talent. Her being able to make people feel better while she played basketball, it was like medicine healing the basketball body and mind.

She has that gift of love for basketball to spread around the world. She knows in her heart that she has tapped into something that is much bigger than herself and try to make people happy by giving them the best show ever based on hard work of training and practicing.

Because of the hard work, Crissa has been able, during a women's basketball games, to give the audience what they have never witness before from a female basketball player who loves the game of basketball. He would always watch her play, and she would show all of her skills on the floor to be witnessed by her fans that basketball is a game of fun and skill, and that she had no problem entertaining them.

She wanted her fans to know through her skill and love of the game, deep down inside of her was an entertainer wanting to come out and entertain all who love the game of basketball as she does. So, it was always that moment in time that her love for the game would shine through her ball handling skills.

CHAPTER TWELVE

IVERSENA
THE BALL HANDLER

There is a very short story behind the young beautiful, loving girl called Iversena, whom this chapter is all about, she is a young beautiful girl that can command and demand the basketball to do things that most males and females on the planet can't do.

A lot of ball players will never be able to spin both balls at the same time with one finger with each hand. Iversena is one of the few young females today on the planet that can demand and command from every male and female the respect as a ball handler in the game called basketball.

Let me tell you a little about the young girl called Iversena. She was a young beautiful female basketball star, in her own mind and heart while growing up. She was a person with the heart and mind of Allen Iverson. Having his ability to handle and shoot the ball was her only goal at that time in her life.

It was the love for the ball that drove her heart to want to be one of the best ball handlers at that time and still today. Iversena is fired up with hot skills off the ball handler press. Daddy personally had the opportunity to experience how this young girl came to be known in her young adolescence years as Iversena the female ball handler.

He is talking about from the age of ten to the age of fifteen. Daddy watched a young girl who wanted to be a basketball star, she mature with certain ball-handling skills. No one on the planet earth could do with the ball what she has done with the ball at her early years of practicing long hours of ball handling.

He watched her change from Crissa Jackson to a known legend in her known world to call herself Iversena. The boys were at awe when he took her to the uptown camp curtain YMCA, they would literally come up to her and ask for her name and then compliment her.

The same thing would happen when she went downtown to the YMCA where the boys and girls would see her in action and would ask her how did she learned to handle the basketball like that, and she would just smile and keep on playing.

Everywhere she would go no one expected to see that kind of handling from a young girl who was not trying to attract attention. She was really shy, she knew that she stood out like someone who is doing a commerical when she starts handling that ball.

It was during the time in Crissa life when she moved to Pennsylvania and started to play school basketball for the first time, in the state of California, they did not have girls' basketball at elementary schools.

While she was playing basketball for her school in the state of Pennsylvania, she would always hear about Allen Iverson and how he became the star for the seventy-sixers, and she would always talk about him as though he was her famous basketball player. She looked up to him as an example of one of the greatest ball handler.

He started taking notice that she was not only talking about him, but she was practicing all of Iverson's basketball drills and moves while talking about him with excitement. Every day during practice and training on and off the court or track, she would always show me that she can do the Iverson ball-handling moves.

So, like a good trainer, dad incorporated her practice of Iverson's ball-handling into her training. He even extended it by telling her that Iverson use to carried his ball with him wherever he went, and "if you are going to be as good as Iverson, than you are going to have to carry your ball with you wherever you go.

You are going to have to dribble your ball on the streets as you are walking so you can learn how to get that control to have better ball handling skills." So, it didn't matter to her where she would go, she would take her ball with her even at school.

He noticed when they were out and about, not training, she would dribble her ball everywhere, and they would stop somewhere, she would sit down and dribble the ball between her legs, around her legs constantly.

After a year or more of that, it came to him that she needed a basketball name, and he came up with that name called Iversena. When he gave her that name, she blew up in her mind and heart, because she was working very hard to have handles like Iverson, and she really liked dad calling her Iversena.

It was after that period dad started introducing her wherever she went as Iversena, and everyone would notice her ball-handling skills that she had work so hard to accomplish. It was during that time that she was getting involved into People to People Ambassador Program for juniors, to be able to go to other countries and represent the United States in basketball.

Iversena had the opportunity to fly to Holland and bring back the MVP and made daddy so proud that he started to call her Iversena all the time, but the older she got, she started to humble herself in the presence of her school team mates, knowing that Iversena was not her real name.

As Iversena, she began to travel all over Pennsylvania to point guard camps, AAU teams and Five-Star Basketball Camps, experiencing the joy and happiness that came from the game of basketball. You can get great results when you love the game from the inside out and the outside in.

Daddy noticed later that she preferred him to call her Crissa instead of Iversena, and to him, that was no problem at all so he began to call her Crissa like he did before. But deep down in his heart, he knew that Iversena would always be in her heart because of the Iverson era.

If you today would mention the name of Iversena, you would see a smile or grin come on her face, that would take her back in the days when dribbling the ball was everything to her. It was a time when Iverson had a lot to do with her basketball behavior as Iversena.

This was a special time when Iversena and the ball became one and lived happy ever after and Crissa began to serve the world the love of the ball handler. Believe it or not, one day they say that Iversena will appear before millions of people displaying her ball handling skills.

CHAPTER THIRTEEN

BURN BABY BURN

This is something her dad believes that the lord has given to him about his little girl who has become his big girl, now involved in the social media industry. It's whenever he listens to or follows social media, he hears and feels his big girl has caused something to start happening inside of social media, it is like a love fire shed up in her bones.

This love fire begins to reveal to him that his big girl is on fire. As he continues to listen to Alicia Keys song "That Girl Is on Fire," he is constantly reminded of the love path that his big girl chosen years ago in order to become a hot love star.

He really feels compelled to travel down this path concerning the singing artist, which is, according to Encarta Dictionary: English (North American English), a person who has the technique of producing musical sounds with their voice, or the performance of songs.

In this chapter he thinks there is a special message in Alicia Keys song, "this girl is on fire" has touch his heart as concerning she a big girl now, "this girl is on fire." He feels that this is the perfect time to connect the song with his big girl that burns, baby, burns.

In this chapter, daddy wanted to be able to share with you his interpretation of what he thinks God is saying spiritually though this song, sung by the great artist Alicia Keys. Like most things in life, you would think that a person would put true love first in what they sing about like Alicia Keys.

He would like to take this time to thank Alicia Keys for her messages in her song, "This Girl Is on Fire," for some reason, most artists leave out the love meaning, emotion and feeling about true love. One writer shared, that in everything you do or say, you should have love in it, and he was not talking about the love of the flesh.

Remember that the writer of the book of First John stated that God is love; think about that for a moment. The reason why he is bringing this up, all music should be about true love, whether or not the person has true love.

The purpose of true love is to bring out your feelings and emotions by way of expressing oneself to another from the heart. Truly, love was design by God and sent out to accomplish everything he sent it out to do in the heart of a man or a woman.

This is one of the reasons why he is writing this chapter because he wants to share with the world that his big girl right now is on fire with the love of the game called basketball. She wants to share herself with the world through social media.

He wants to tell the world that he received revelation that Alicia Keys is God song messenger. She is reaching the nation of the United States with love that will change the heart and lives of her audience all over the world.

He would like to introduce to some and present to others a brand-new way of writing spiritually about the music artists in the industry. This will be something new and fresh like you have never seen or heard before in the history of yesterday, today, and the future.

He would like to take this time in this chapter to share with you his version of "This Girl Is on Fire" by one of the greatest artist of all time, wonderful, beautiful, and spiritual "Alicia Keys." Before he gets started, he would like to share something that is very important to him when he listens or looks at Alicia Keys, he sees and hears the message to "daddy's big girl" now.

He like to mention that he has a daughter who he believes looks almost identical to Alicia Keys when they are not standing side by side, she even smiles, laughs and talks like Alicia Keys. Daddy knows you will say the same thing when you see the both of them on social media, especially when the both of them are doing their thing as an entertainer.

His daughter name is Crissa Jackson, the one and only thirteenth female to be inducted into the greatest basketball team of all times called "The Harlem Globe Trotters." If you really want to compare her with Alicia Keys, then you can just look up her name, Crissa Jackson, on the internet or social media.

He just wanted to take this time to write about daddy's big girl, who can exemplify (be characterize) every word that Alicia Keys is singing in that song "This Girl Is on Fire." Now he wants you to know that God has given him this charge to write about daddy's big girl who is on fire.

The way God gave it to him makes a lot of sense to him right now, because his big girl is all about the love of being fire up and it is his mission to try to help you understand how daddy's little girl is now all grown up and fire up with love.

Pictures of
Crissa Jackson and Alicia Keys

He will try to commit himself to write something after each paragraph concerning Alicia Keys songs. Have you ever been in a situation where you felt that "no one" can make you feel the way you are feeling?

The only answer he had was for you to read this book and you will discover, what Crissa discover about the power of God's love in the sport world of your choice. He believes his big girl is connected to the messages of Alicia Keys songs.

She wants to spread that love fire over the world by showing and telling everyone she is on fire and not just any kind of fire, her fire is a love fire, and in this chapter, he will try with all of his heart to interpret and relate Alicia Keys message to the world.

He would like to use Alicia Keys songs to share his spiritual twist of what he thinks it is saying about daddy's little girl who is a big girl now and is on fire with love. He gives all respect and credit to Alicia Keys and songwriters: Jeff Bhasker, Alicia Augello-Cook, Salaam Remi, Billy Squire, Nicki Minaj © Sony/ATV Music Publishing LLC, Universal Music Publishing Group, Spirit Music Group.

She just a girl and she's on fire, Hotter than a fantasy, lonely like a highway. She's living in a world and it's on fire filled with catastrophe but she knows she can fly away oh, oh, oh, oh, oh, she got both feet on the ground and she's burning it down oh, oh, oh, oh, oh.

Like he told you, he was inspired by her song because it reminds him of his big girl now. He really thinks and believes that Alicia Keys was singing about herself, trying to give herself as a message to the world that every girl can be on fire.

Alicia Keys wanted to reveal the fire in her life at this point, and he needed to share with you and the world about daddy's big girl and how she is fired up with a new kind of fire that is called "Love Fire." He really felt that the world needs to know about the kind of love fire that his big girl is bringing to social media.

He is so happy that his big girl is bringing a love fire that is known for putting out negative fires that would try to come against her career, and this chapter is to let the world know about this kind of fire of love.

Alicia Keys has a two-fold message, and daddy wanted to take a step of faith and try to interpret that message of double power. The power of love is to be energized as love energy, helping her to move forward, pressing on to success and victory.

The power to love as fire has the ability to turn the light in one's heart to excel, finding your way to stardom and fame. In this book, written in this chapter is a thank-you going out to Alicia Keys in love and much prayer that would continue to empower her with the ability to be able to produce more of God's love fire.

He hopes and prays that Alicia Keys continues to receive God's love as fire. This love was created and designed personally by God for daddy's big girl to be able to succeed in the social media world with her love fire. You must understand about the spiritual interpretation of this kind of fire that is fueled by love.

He knows that the Holy Spirit will give you the revelation of the true love power of God as fire, so you would be able to use fire as a method to express his love in the hearts of men and women all over the world.

This kind of fire of love is true and real, when you are sharing it with the social media world, you will be expressing yourself from your heart and the heart of God. Daddy wants you to know that a love fire is a type or symbol of the spiritual power of energy that lights up a person's heart with true love.

Again, this kind of love fire is going to spread like wild fire throughout the social media industry. You can't fake or pretend to have this kind of love, it is God's love, which is a spiritual ball of love energy of light.

A love fire is a bright light that shines in darkness and through social media for the entire world to see. All he is trying to say is that Alicia Keys and Crissa Jackson have the same kind of love fire that can only be received from God only, and if you are planning to have a love fire like they have, then you need to know God first in the pardon of your sins.

Alicia Keys has a two-fold message as was stated earlier in this chapter, the second one is, she has been gifted from God to reach her followers naturally and spiritually. He hopes from this chapter you will be able to see the love call from God to Alicia Keys when you listen to her music.

She got her head in the clouds and she's not backing down, this girl is on fire, this girl is on fire, she's walking on fire, this girl is on fire, looks like a girl, but she's a flame so bright, she can burn your eyes. Better look the other way, you can try but you'll never forget her name, she's on top of the world hottest of the hottest girls say oh, oh, oh, oh, oh.

He would like to bring to your attention to what he believes her message is trying to say to Crissa. Stay focused with no distraction while you are looking to heaven full of energy, and her eyes begins to light up as fire causing her whole body to become flames. You can only look at her from a distance as she becomes the hottest commodity in the social media industry through love of basketball.

In other words, Alicia Keys has always looked to God from where her blessings come from and finally received the baptism of the Holy Spirit, which empowered her to write and sing until she transformed spiritually into a ball of fire lighting up the music industry.

He believes that Alicia Keys message has shed some fire on his big girl, because she is soaring with the eagles mentally, physically, and spiritually and not with the pigeons, she is pressing toward the love mark of great success. Crissa Jackson is walking on water, walking through the fire with her torch and her eyes are like the flames of love.

As Alicia Keys stated in her song that she is the world's hottest of the hottest girls, he would like to add that his big girl is the hottest love fire and willing by faith to walk through the fire and not be moved by what she sees or feels, but by what the Holy Spirit shows her in the love fire.

Remember the story of the three Hebrew boys who were thrown into the fiery furnace, to discover that there was a fourth person who was the "Son of God," this story will remind you how powerful is the love fire that is in your heart.

Crissa Jackson is burning with so much love fire and love energy that it's consumes up everything that gets in her way, everything that tries to distract her from getting all of her breaks. Crissa has worked so hard coming up through the ranks of success that she gives all the credit to the love of the game.

The reason why she was on fire, she was told to go into Jesus's vineyard as a type of track and court, and train, practice and whatever is right, he would paid her. He wants you to pay close attention to the words whatever is right.

Crissa will receive the right acting video, right commercials, right ball-handling contract, right following on social media, and the right career and success, because of God's love fire in her heart. All he has to say about Crissa is "Burn Baby Burn!

Alicia is right about this world, it can be very lonely, causing you to feel lonely. Thank God that never happen to daddy's big girl, especially now that she has the main ingredient called true love fire, she is fueled with spiritual energy that will never leave her or forsake her, it will keep her feet on the ground running.

His point is that God's love fire will never leave you; all you have to do is seek his love for what you are planning to do for your life. You are going to have to love God with all of your heart, mind, strength, and soul if you want to have love fire.

Alicia Keys message to him and his big girl is that she is just more than just a girl; she is a big girl that is on fire spreading that spiritual love energy all over the world. This love fire of Crissa is going to take the advantage of every opportunity to accomplish and achieve her plans, goals, and vision through social media.

Remember, Crissa is working on the love flames to be able to have insight in the sport industry and social media. In other words, it is said spiritually that in the year 2020 everyone can experience sight beyond sight to see the bigger picture with foresight into her future with social media.

This book was written so the world could become involved with Crissa through social media every day. It's not that the world of social media won't be able to see her soaring like an eagle on fire with flaming eyes, but everyone will have all the opportunity to engage her true beauty on the inside as her love fire burns baby burn.

Just remember that only God's love can give you a true love fire that can't be quenched or stopped. If you need to have this kind of love fire, all you have to do is give your heart, mind, body, and strength to God.

You know the drill; all you have to do is ask Jesus to come into your heart as Savior and Lord. According to Second Corinthians 5:17, you will become a new creation. This will open up heaven and give you the opportunity to burn, baby, burn with God's love fire!

SECTION FOUR

Crissa the Big Girl
Part 4
True Love that Serves

THE HEART OF A SERVANT

W hen all the dust clears the air and the runner hits the ground, you have to know that you are running to win and get your prize. Whatever sport you chose you got to serve that sport as a servant. You got to know that you are really in love with the sport of your choice.

His girl was truly an entertainer, but way down in her heart she knew that she is serving the public and her fans because of love. How to be a servant is one of the most important things when you pick out a sport that you love.

You have to decide in your heart to be one of the best players, that serves your sport of choice. In order for a person to grow in a sport, they must serve their sport through dedication and commitment. You are required by love to train hard and serve the love of the game, in order for you to serve the people.

There are two very important points that he needed to share with you about love. The importance of these two is each one should be a part of your foundation (principles and concepts) while you building, training and practicing to serve the love of the game.

First, you can't serve basketball or football at the same time, thinking that you are going to be great at them both. You are going to have to decide in your heart, if it is going to be the one or the other. It is going to take everything in you to fall in love with just one. Remember, you have to be true and love the one your with.

In other words, you've got to fall in love with the one that you can give all of you. That is a principle, and the second, it is going to take the whole person to learn to serve with all of your mind, heart and body to become a servant of love to the sport of your choice.

You heard of the saying, "let the greatest among you be the servant," if you are planning to be great in your choice of sport, you need to continue to read this book with compassion and always be focusing on serving the sport you love.

Many people have heard this saying before, "train up a child the way that they should go and when they get older they will not depart from the truth, the training or the teaching." He wants you to know that every parent's first responsibility when God gives them a child as a gift, you have to give that gift back to God for his blessing to be on your child.

That's how Crissa life began in the Jackson's family, she was given to them by God for a purpose with a destiny, and it was their responsibility to make sure they fulfilled that duty as parents by giving her back to God for covering, protection, and security.

This is how they gave her back to God; first they dedicated her back to God spiritually, so that his blessing would be on them and her to be able to follow the leading of the Holy Spirit. He understood his first priority with her was to train her up mentally, physically and spiritually so she would be able to do God's will in her life.

Their responsibility as a husband-wife team was to give her fair opportunity to journey into her life with no fear, dad knew that God's perfect love would cast out all fear. What that means, is that she would not live in fear, but in the love of God.

He knew early in her life, the fear of the world had to be cast out, rebuke, driven out, expelled according to Hebrew 5:12. His purpose was to share, teach or preach the words of love as seeds to be sow and planted down inside of her heart.

In other words, when the love seeds of God traveled down on the inside of the heart of Crissa, it was from him speaking love words directly to her, you have to understand that love has a mission to perform for God down inside of the heart of Crissa when it comes to being a servant of love.

This is a good time to help you understand the importance of God's words of love and action serving on and off the track and court. Once you apply faith through love, you have to serve it by speaking and doing in the sports of your choice.

The word of God starts as the spirit of God and is carried by words that are transformed into the heart of Crissa, and that is where God begins to speak to her about the things concerning her ability to serve in every capacity for the love of the sport

Please pay close attention to this statement; once that love word gets to where it needs to be inside of Crissa heart, it begins to turn the Holy Spirit on to all negative and positive thoughts and intent that will try to hinder or build the servant in her to love the game.

His point is about the love word of God and how it is building Crissa personality and character along the way of her love journey to serve basketball and social media. He hopes you have learned how the Holy Spirit drives all the negative thoughts out by love, and he wants you to look up that scripture (Hebrews 4:12) so you can verify the truth of about God's word.

So, he began to train Crissa to serve basketball through God in everything, one day, she will have to give back what God had given her to all the people she comes into contact with on her journey through sports and social media.

All this is possible for Crissa, she has dedicated and committed her life to the love of the game. He hopes you can see, a servant only leads you to serve others who are searching for the love of the game of basketball in life.

The reason behind this ideal (preparing Crissa for service through love) or concept (a group of ideas about how you can become a servant of love) is to prepare you if you are going to try to succeed in life no matter who you are.

He knows that you are going to need to learn about God's love and how to serve that love, without God's love you will not have a chance in life. What you don't understand about these principles is they work in a person life who is seeking love.

The teaching he shared about his little girl was for you to learned how to love and served the game called basketball. You have to let that love draw you to the greater cause that serves the people by making them happy, laughing, and excited about the love of the game and life.

This will be the most interesting time of your career, you need to use your gift or talent for the service of love if you are going to continue in sports and finish your destiny. Once you have learned how to serve love, love has no problem serving you to become successful and great.

According to, "sound spiritual doctrine" on the teachings of the concepts of love truths, Crissa will continual to be more affective during her course of training and practicing social media. The "secret" of getting love to serve you, is for you to serve love.

There is no way that anyone can get around not serving love and succeed, you got to love whatever it is that you want to become or do in life. Love requires that you first build by laying a foundation down in your heart.

In other words, you have to repent, believe, confess, and accept his love salvation, and only then you will take on the new nature of love. Now you might not have been ready to hear this, but God is love, and those who want or need his love have to come through Jesus Christ.

She confessed her Christianity because the bible said that all people were to go into all the world and share the love of God, and he or she that believes shall be saved and those that don't shall be condemned.

She was taught to pray for her ability to comprehend her education. She was taught to respect all adults or elderly people. She was taught to treat all people with caring love, because that was the teaching of her lord and savior Jesus Christ.

Teaching and training her spiritually was a very easy task, she was able to incorporate into her life education, family, and sport. She had to contend with a father and mother who oversee their own church ministry throughout her years of growing.

She never had any other pastor but her father to train her to serve the spiritual love work of God and how to incorporate it into the love of the game and social media. As she got older, her understanding became broader, she understood what he was doing as a servant for God, he was serving God, the family, church family, and Crissa at first hand every day.

He explained to his little girl that he was serving her in the name of the lord, as a servant, and "one day, you will have to serve him through the love of the game or social media if this is going to be your life." He knew something that everyone did not know about her, that she loved basketball like she loved God.

He knew that his little girl was going to work together with God like one, hand in hand one day in the future. He knew there was going to be an anointing on her life because of her dedication, loyalty, commitment, and faithfulness in which all stems from the love of God that is rooted deeply and richly in her heart.

Crissa served basketball like she was trained to serve God, he made sure that she incorporate the love of God into her training, that's the only way she was going to be a basketball star. Her life dependent on her to serve the love of the game.

The bible says in the book of 1 Corinthians 2:9, "eyes have not seen and ears have not heard about the things that God has instore for them that love and are called according to his purpose," especially when it comes to serving sports.

Sometimes, you can't see the future, but you know you can sense that God is in control and that his plan will prevail. You have to understand this truth that God watches over his word to perform it, and his word of love will never fail by returning to him void, but it will accomplish everything that God sent it out to do in Crissa and you.

Can this be your prayer too? As she kept training and giving God the glory every year, you could see God was doing something in her life to show her that it was him opening the doors for her to serve. You must remember that daddy and his little girl were just ordinary people who knew no one, having no money and prestige, but still pursued the love of the game.

Daddy and his little girl could not put themselves in front of anybody who could advance their situation. It was from the muscle, through the tussle, that they had to hustle in order to learn to serve the love of the game.

Crissa was fully aware of their situation and knew that she had to work hard physically, mentally, and spiritually. This was her task at hand, she had to prove to God and her daddy that she was up for the task and ready for all challenges.

One thing that they both knew, all they had for support was the Father God, Son Jesus, and the Holy Spirit. No other help they knew, but to pray and fast during most of the times when they did not know where to go and what to do to train and practice.

They were learning early to depend on his word and to wait for the next move or direction. Never despise new beginnings, it is where the love of God really shows up for you. He wants to give you the best lessons and spiritual education that you need to receive from this book from the early years of Crissa training and practicing.

One specific thing he figured out about Crissa early in her journey, she would travel during her growing pains of learning and gathering. His interpretation was based on his experience, it revealed to him that she has been called like her daddy to the life of true love.

The difference between her and him, she will travel all over the world, spreading God's love like she been trained to do, and her daddy will serve love as a writing evangelist, writing books of love, spreading it all over the world.

He would relate to her by serving her as an example of serving love as a father, in the future he will write books about love to serve the world. He truly started his training with Crissa with this teaching in mind, that God so love the world that he gave his son Jesus and he gave him Crissa.

Also, his son Jesus loved you so much that he too gave his life so that you can do what his teaching is revealing to you to do for your child. Please, learn how to speak and show love in the sport of your choice.

In other words, he became that love vessel to her and sacrificed himself for her career, so she too one day would sacrifice herself for the world by showing and sharing the love of God through basketball. The bible says in the book of Jeremiah 31:3, "with loving kindness I have drawn you."

He knew, love would be the center of attraction for her to do whatever she needed to do in life, and he is talking on the court, about defense and offense, and off the court, showing love with her personality and character.

The bible says, love is God, and Jesus said that everyone needs to love the lord your God with all of your heart, mind, soul, and strength. To love your neighbors as you love yourself. He discovered and shared with Crissa that love is the answer to all things, and everything you do, you need to do it in love, especially basketball.

Daddy will continue to help you learn, love is one of the only powers and forces that are drawing people to God, sports, and each other spiritually. Now that you're done trying everything else, now it is time to try God's love.

What is needed to be re-enforced so you would really know and understand that the concept of love is a spiritual mystery, a place in the natural mind where human love is unknown, love is spiritual and you need it for sports.

He hopes this is clear to you, if you do anything without love, you will not prosperous spiritually while you train and practice in the real world, you will be beating and swinging in the air, missing everything spiritually with your words and actions.

Out of your mouth will come nothing without love, even though you think that you are sharing, reaching, teaching, and working on your vision spiritually, still you will fail. Without love, you will accomplish nothing.

You have not planned to fail, you have fail to plan, you will end up in life with nothing of spiritual value, you did not plan to play, you play to fail your daughter or son in the love sport of their choice. You got to man and woman up for this task.

You are daddy's little girl or mommy's little boy, and you have to give up everything to pick up your love cross to follow the game of sports. Daddy has given his little girl all the love that he could mustard up, getting from God all he could get.

Crissa is now fired up, tested up, rested up, filled up, and getting up to share the love of God where ever she's goes in life with her ball handling skills. She has accepted all of her daddy's love and teaching on love as part of her training and practicing to become successful in the lifestyle of love through social media.

He thinks she is going to be one of God's greatest love servants of all times while she is serving in the world of basketball and business through social media. She already knows that she need to use her hard working ethics.

She worked so hard on her love for ball handling, more practicing than talking; now she will demonstrate God's love through her gift from God as the ball handler. If you ever go see her do anything dealing with the ball, watch the love come through her like you have never seen or witnessed before.

What you are seeing is the love of a servant who has been prepared for this from her mother's womb and was trained by the daddy, Crissa the servant, is to share the Lord's love to the whole wide world through basketball. Truly, she is daddy's little girl who is becoming a love servant to the world of social media.

CHAPTER FIFTEEN

BABY DADDY

He felt that you would be wondering what is a "baby daddy" and what is it all about? He wanted to insert a twist in this chapter that would get your attention about the baby daddy. A daddy, according to the Urban Dictionary, is the kind of man that is worthy of a lot of beautiful babies, because of his meaning and purpose in life.

A daddy can produce strong intelligent babies full of love and loyal devotion to him for his whole life. His loving kindness is unconditional and selfless toward all his babies, the way God's love intended for a daddy's love to be for his baby.

Daddy will kiss the skin-bruised knees to make them better and speak sweet words of healing and will nurse the colds with prayer and faith. A daddy will work physically to satisfy his baby physical and emotional needs, no matter if it rains, snows, or shine, daddy will always be on time.

A daddy will share with his baby nice things when the baby is sad and will make the baby feel beautiful when mad. If the baby is feeling lonely, a daddy will put in the quality time just to give enough love that God has given him for the baby only.

A daddy is the kind of man that will correct his baby girl in the spirit of love, especially when the baby is out of control. Daddy would share his love with his baby boy, causing him to feel better afterwards. A daddy is not only a man in love with his baby, but the baby will become his best friend.

He is the kind of daddy that will always nurture his baby's character on the inside and flow with the personality on the outside, as the baby grows from a caterpillar to a beautiful gorgeous butterfly of love. Remember beauty is in the eyes and heart of the beholder.

The daddy will go out of his way to make his baby feel safe and protected, growing up in a social society with nothing but social media, daddy will give his baby confidence and the ability of empowerment. A daddy teaches and inspires his baby to love at the top of their ability in whatever they decided to do in life.

That daddy is able to transfer that love into the lives of his babies. He is also the kind of daddy that will search his own heart to find what it takes to please his baby and would never, ever abuse sexually, mistreat, or take the advantage of his baby body and mind.

Daddy would not take his sweet, caring, and loving baby for granted, his love is unconditionally, uncompromised, unlimited, and spiritual. Daddy's love is the kind of love that would sacrifice for the good of his baby.

A true loving daddy will always try to find a way to show patience, kindness, wisdom, strength, sweetness, fun, sensuality, intelligence, caring, respect, gentleness, and prudence with love to his baby. A true loving daddy, will become that all-amazing one of a kind daddy that will never ever leave her side.

The kind of daddy you dream about as being your daddy for real and never ever ending up with a fake, fraud, phony, substitute, or negative example of a daddy. This is why daddy baby must grow up to be his little girl or little boy who has a love for sports.

If you are not a daddy baby, learn very quickly how to pray, fast, and fight for the kind of daddy that is worth fighting for, worth praying for, worth waiting for to love. Whether he is biological or adopted daddy, it shouldn't matter, he will be given to you by God himself.

A God-given and sent daddy will always be there for his baby at their best interest in every area of their life. In any event that he can't be there for his babies physically, mentally, or socially, he will never give up the love fight to be there.

A true, honest, and devoted daddy, when he leaves the presences of his baby, he will never leave them spiritually because God's Spirit is always presence to aid, protect, and secure his baby. A smart daddy would always find a way to invest in his baby's future financially, and if he is spiritually smart, he would invest in their spiritual welfare of the future.

Because of his love for his baby, he will make sure that he invests into the earthly and heavenly banks with interest. Daddy knows when it comes to his baby; he can't leave any stones up turned, so he makes sure that he made provision for his baby to be able to always receive what they need even when he get older.

A daddy's love will always be in the heart of his baby and the baby in the heart of her daddy, and they will never leave each other's hearts, their hearts will always remind them that their love will never fail each other.

This will always give hope and beliefs, together they will endure all things, because the baby will always be daddy's little girl or boy. Are you the daddy, taking your good oh time showing love? Well, he hopes you are the one that is reading this chapter concerning your baby.

You know that just making babies is not about having sex, getting woman pregnant is all about creating life and receiving gifts from God. Also, it is taking responsibility for your actions and reactions. Daddy, this is a call to you to stop thinking about yourself and begin to think about your baby or babies.

Did you know that your baby or babies are praying from their heart(s) to God, hoping you would be there for them as their daddy? It is time for you to start focusing on their lives and their future because they need their daddy.

There is so much that the daddy can feel when it comes to his baby's pain and hear in his heart the cry throughout this chapter and even some writing in this book about daddy's little girl, who is Crissa Ann Jackson, known as "The "Ace of Spades."

He can see your babies spiritually reaching out figuratively, mentally, verbally, literally and spiritually to you by way of a broken heart and a contrite spirit, they suffer from despair, desertion, and not getting your love.

He believes and hopes that the God of love will draw the daddy back into the lives of his babies or draw him back into the relationship that he once had with his babies. The call goes out again, this is your time to pick up the broken pieces.

He hopes this book has given daddy the window of opportunity and the door of another chance to enter into a new relationship or a reviving one with all of his babies. He believes that you are having a hard time mustering up the strength to do what you know is right for your baby.

He believes the next best thing that would probably give or help you with a new start with your baby is to pull your life together. Is it possible, that this could be your turning point that you must face in order to face your baby?

If you think that you need help from God in order to do this task or take on this mission, if you choose to do so, he would like to take this time to introduce Jesus the fixer, the miracle worker, and the baby daddy restorer.

If you would like to pray with me or on your own, Jesus would come into your heart and save you and fill you with his love spirit to be able to have a relationship with your babies, you can also tell Jesus that you want to begin your journey right now.

It is now time for God to help you to contact or research the where about of any of your babies might be right now. Remember that Jesus is a way maker, and he is able to do exceedingly above and beyond what you are able to do especially in this kind of situation.

That's why it is important for you to take these steps toward making it right in your life, you are the "baby daddy." This is your open door or window to choose God's love to act on the fact, that the baby needs her daddy.

CHAPTER SIXTEEN

THE LOVE FRONTIER

Welcome to the open love frontier of this book, this is about Crissa Jackson and her daddy, he wanted to save the best for the last chapters, so let's open up this chapter with a blast. This book is a true love story of Crissa Jackson which includes all of her history and memories that her fans and followers through social media need to know.

People do not know about the true love that perform miracles during Crissa journey to become a star in basketball. What dad has done in this book was to fill in all the information that you might need to know about Crissa, he also invites you can take the same personal journey as she did in the sports world.

The author hopes and believes that he has taken care of most of the things in Crissa life that shows the evidence and facts of a "True Love Story" in this book. Some people would call this book the autobiography of the greatest female baller that ever lived, and her name is Crissa A. Jackson, the ball handler.

The A is the acronym for the word "Ace," which means the thirteenth female to be inducted into the world wide-known Harlem Globe Trotters. This is a world known international professional basketball team and she was the ball handler and that was her name with the jersey number one.

Crissa A. Jackson is her real name and the middle initial A stands for Ann. She is called by her mother and father Crissa Ann when she behaves negative. She never like to be called Ann by anyone, she felt like she was being disrespected or being make fun of as a person.

With appearances on "Good Morning American," "Wendy Williams Show," "To Tell the Truth," "The Rolling Stones," commercial with "Champions," "Dare to Champions," campaign, Under Armour X and Kohl's Commercial, Adidas Women Athlete Commercial, Campaign for Casino, and the hair product "Pantene" and many other appearances, Crissa A. Jackson is moving at a very steady pace through social media.

According to WhatIs.com, social media which is the collective of online communications channels dedicated to community-based input, interaction, content-sharing, and collaboration. He wants to share social media information as it relates to Crissa and her future and how she is learning how to manage social media business concepts on line and off line.

He needs to share with you, how social media has shaped her life in just a few years by giving her support and an opportunity to build a following. Her followers which are creating a very large following throughout social media is an integral part of her life online as relating to all the things she is doing on You Tube and others.

She spends a lot of time developing her network of short films, modeling, making speaking appearance, and training people in basketball and physical workouts along with international basketball games all over the United States

Hopefully this book will help launch Crissa Jackson internationally to travel all over the world and through social media. She is marketing her products and promoting her brands, connects to current customers and foster new business is what she is all about in 2021-2025.

Crissa graduated from Point Loma University with a bachelor degree in business. She is using her experience and knowledge to advance herself through social media by promoting and marketing herself every day to the whole wide world.

Because of her experience with the Harlem Globe Trotters, she has networked on social media like it has never been worked before within three and a half years. According to the Facebook community, Crissa has over three thousand people or more, who like her and climbing and three thousand people who follow what she does every day and still climbing.

Based on the information given by Instagram, Crissa has over five hundred fifty-five posts and still building, as well as a hundred thirty-three thousand followers and seven hundred forty-two who are following her some other way.

Crissa have supporters that will back her on social media which gives her motivation to keep moving forward and growing. You can email Crissa Jackson at: book@crissajackson.com youtu. be/77vJv-QKMUE. She is a Pro Baller, A Moment With Crissa the Entertainer,• Influencer,• Host,• Model,• Actress,• Trainer,• and Motivational Speaker.

For bookings, email her at: book@crissajackson.com, Based on Tweets' current page, Crissa has 1,006 following, 1775 followers, and 4336 likes and steady growing very fast day by day. You need to check Crissa out on youtube.com/crissajackson because she is doing big things, and you can check her out @samayacg doing big things and @picklerandben as soon as you can!

Retweeted Crissa Jackson @WORLDSTAR #wshh#world-star#WorldStarHiphop. Remember when you're trying to get fit and you need a tip, contact Crissa Jackson because she can and will get you to be equipped. In other words, she will get you prepared and ready to work real steady, and before you know it, you will be ready to rock steady with Crissa A.

Daddy knows that she is the best in the North, East, South, and the West, all over the world of sports. This is an interview by Syreeta McFadden on April 18, 2017 about Crissa Jackson. A small boy rocking a yarmulke can hardly deal with the excitement.

An even smaller voice, from a young girl with short pigtails, escapes the din of the crowd: "Where is Ace?" "She sports the signature blue, red and headband of the team. Her dad points to the edge of the court, toward the fiery Ace Jackson, the Harlem point guard, who is buoyantly rallying the crowd as Dizzy makes the team's final attempt to seal a lead before the clock runs out.

Crissa "Ace" Jackson was one of four women who grace the roster of one of the oldest basketball clubs in the world. It's a record in the long history of the Harlem Globetrotters. At five-foot-four, she reminds longtime lovers of the game of Charlotte Hornets" point guard Muggsy Bogues.

She is swift and slick, and, on the court playing with exclusively men, that swiftness serves her well. Jackson, twenty-seven, who grew up in California and moved to Pennsylvania, credits her daddy for shaping her into the ballplayer that she is today.

Her daddy once scoffed at the idea, told her she was ""too small,"" and Jackson threatened to tell her mother. Jackson retells this story with humor and pride. She took to the sport when she was six years old and never looked back.

"My dad used to call me "Iversina," she says with a laugh. Jackson studied a lot of players, but paid close attention to Alan Iverson legendary crossover move when she was in junior high by watching DVDs her daddy brought, to support her innate talent and enthusiasm for the sport.

Jackson's father played some street ball but responded to his daughter charge to train her in the game with enthusiasm even after she ratted him out to her mom. In return, Jackson opted out of middle school trips to the mall to train year-round, immersing herself in training videos and perfecting her version of Iverson crossover dribble.

I love the dribble. I love doing ball handling stuff, which is why I fit with the Globetrotters so well."" The young fans get a taste of that magical ball handling when her teammate passes Ace the ball once the starters are introduced to giddy fans.

The Globetrotters twerk, dab and spin balls on their fingertips as their signature tune, the "Brother Bones," "Sweet Georgia Brown," fills the stadium. Commented in the first half of the game, Ace sinks not one, but two 4-point shots.

The crowd goes wild. It was the Globetrotters that created the 3-point field goal in the early days of professional basketball games. Ace is aware of what this moment means to young girls and boys who watch this 5-foot-4 phenome player that can run with big boys.

This is a personal note from her daddy; there is no man or woman today that he knows about that can spin two balls at one time but "Daddy's Little Girl" Crissa Ace Jackson." With the team during the Harlem Globetrotters game at Barclays Center on April 2nd, 2017.

Crissa is fully equipped with the full package of God's love, having the ability to express the joy of the lord with the intensity of happiness which takes her to a spiritual zone of comfort when handling the ball.

This kind of excitement and expression only flows through the power of the love of the game of basketball, and not too many people have the opportunity or know how to enter into that love zone of basketball.

This is another article written by Matthew Florjancic published at 3:58 p.m. eastern time on January 5, 2017 concerning Crissa Jackson. In less than two years, Crissa "Ace" Jackson has gotten to do far more than she ever thought possible in the game of basketball, she has made good decision to attend a tryout with the Harlem Globetrotters.

Dad wants you to remember that your gift will make room for you and the love of God will draw opportunities to you and that same love will give you a drive that will take you all the way to your success and destiny.

Crissa Jackson has gotten to see 12 foreign countries and entertain millions of loyal fans as part of the 2017 World Tour for the Globetrotters, who have celebrated their 91st consecutive year of bringing their unique brand of basketball to every corner of the earth.

He shared with you earlier that Crissa was given a charge by God that she was going to travel the world and shared the love of God and you can witness that for yourself by the news reports and interviews. "It's an amazing experience being the 13th female to play for the Harlem Globetrotters in 91 years," Ace said on a recent trip to Cleveland.

"It's being able to put smiles on people's faces, being a role model to the young females, and sometimes, even the young boys. It's a dream come true. "It's more than I thought I would ever be able to do in life.

You always grow up thinking, 'What is your purpose here?' And I always thought it was just to play basketball competitively, but now, I'm able to play competitively and be that role model and ambassador of goodwill.

It's just so amazing to make an impact in life." Jackson says, the impact she is able to make with her talents on the court and goodwill visits away from the game lifts her spirits, despite whatever challenges are provided by being away from family and friends during long tours throughout the United States and in other countries.

"Everything has its pros and cons, but these pros outweigh the cons," Jackson said. "I'm away from home, not around my family, but I'm still able to bring that joy to other families, and that brings joy to me.

If I'm going through something that day, they really bring me up. Whatever they're going through that day, I'm able to bring them up. It's like a partnership and something we can all actually enjoy together. "I always wanted to play professional basketball.

I've been playing sinced seven years old and started training at the age of six years old, I had an opportunity for a tryout with the Globetrotters, and not only now am I playing professional basketball, I'm traveling the world. I'm putting smiles on millions of people's faces, helping them have a good time, family entertainment.

"We're goodwill ambassadors, so now, we're actually able to go to hospitals and put smiles on people's faces who aren't able to come to the games, go and talk to kids about bullying prevention. There's a lot of perks to being a Harlem Globetrotter."

Known as "Ace" by fans and teammates alike, Jackson is determined to continue building up her game in order to entertain the millions of Globetrotter supporters around the world. "I'm always striving to be the best in everything that I do," Jackson said.

"I'm always training. When I was young, I was always on the track running or always dribbling a basketball, always carrying a basketball. It's because, I have so much drive to be the best at what I'm doing, and that's why I'm able to give to the game.

"I'm a great dribbler. I have a lot of energy. I need somewhere to put it. What better place to be than on the court, something I love doing, and that's what I'm passionate about. I'm able to do that with the Globetrotters."

He hopes you will remember the interviews and reporters stories that Crissa shared with you about her experience with the Harlem Globe Trotters. Through her interviews and news reporters, she gave you information about how she had to go through to become that person that she saw as a child.

Crissa spoke faith over her own life by calling that which was not, yet manifest as through she had already gotten it. When she said that she was going to be a star, and a star she became by faith through love.

That love produce joy unspeakable and full of glory. This is another article produced by PLNU about alum Crissa Jackson joining the Globe Trotters on October 10, 2015 at 5:00 p.m. San Diego Former Point Loma women basketball player Crissa Jackson (2010-12) has signed a contract to play for the Harlem Globetrotters.

Coming out of their training camp, the Globetrotters signed four new players, including Jackson, for their much-anticipated world tour. Jackson was the only female out of the four signees to join this iconic team that has been providing smiles, sportsmanship and service to millions of people worldwide for over 90 years.

"We can't wait to hit the floor and celebrate our 90th year with families around the world," "said Globetrotters Legend Sweet Lou Dunbar, the team's director of player personnel," "and we are excited about what these outstanding rookies will bring to the court to help us give our wonderful fans memories that will last a lifetime."

The author wants you to know that love created and designed Crissa for the future time of this day and have given her the ability to rise to the occasion, because she is the love entertainer of all time in the basketball world of today.

She is God's gift that will not only put smiles on the kids' faces, but she will send basketball love message to their hearts, she is able to create a very special moment in time that will last for a life time for her fans. Crissa has been prepared by the love of God through training hard and practicing in difficult times.

In her past, she would work and labor very hard to be able to dribble her heart out with joy, laughter, and happiness that will move the people, especially the children, to a new world of joy, fun, and pleasure for the love of the game called "Basketball."

Crissa is a winner and not a loser, she is on top of her game and not on at the bottom, she is the victor in anything that she does with the ball basketball in her hands and not the victim. She will never give up and never give in, nor will she stop loving the game of basketball.

This is a fact, she has seen what the love of basketball can do to millions of people by putting smiles on their faces and love in their hearts for the game called "Basketball." Sports have a message and joy to be delivered by the sport players.

If anyone in the game of basketball can find a way to help millions and millions of people to find hope, peace, joy, and love in the game of basketball, Crissa can, she will become one of the most powerful force of love that draws the people to her love for the game.

Hailing from Harrisburg, Pennsylvania, Crissa "Ace" Jackson is the 13th female player in the history of the Globetrotters, joining current female stars TNT Maddox and Sweet J Ekworomadu. Ace played her first two years of college ball at Savannah State University (Ga.), where she quickly grabbed the starting point guard job as a freshman and led the team in three-pointers and assists

She led the team in scoring and assists as a sophomore and was named to the NCAA Division I All-Independent All-American second team. The 5-4 standout guard then transferred to Point Loma Nazarene University for her final two seasons, leading the Sea Lions in points (15.4 ppg), three-pointers (1.4 3pg) and assists (4.3 ppg) as a junior, and in three-pointers (1.5 3pg), assists (3.8 ppg) and steals (2.7 ppg) as a senior.

Jackson and the rest of the first-year players will join a star-studded roster featuring Hi-Lite Bruton, Big Easy Lofton, Ant Atkinson, Bull Bullard, Cheese Chisholm and Thunder Law, as the Globetrotters will play over 330 games in more than 260 cities in 48 U.S. states, eight Canadian provinces and Puerto Rico from December 26, 2015, through April 2016.

Crissa has discover the social media as a powerful resource in the twenty-first century and her daddy is so proud of her to discover the love train that is going to get her from point A to point B. This love train is her transportation to communicate to the many thousands and millions of people who are going to support her on her love journey to stardom.

He is now beginning to understand that Crissa have a phenomenal following. That means networking businesses can make money off of her, she has an extraordinary following of people, and she is marketable.

He thinks that a new rise of people who been expose to love are beginning to express and show their love for Crissa like they have never expressed a love for anyone who is rising to stardom. This is something new and fresh for the social media world to experience.

The reason is because in one of my other books called "The Royal Love Law" or "The Five Spiritual Love Language," He talks about how you are living in a love dispensation period that is causing people to experience love like they have never before.

He's been given the opportunity to teach and train Crissa to be a love child, and what he means by that is this, he believes that everyone is drawn by love, and love is what makes the world go round and love has everything to do with everything that is happening in the twenty first century.

In other words, God spoke and said with loving kindness, "I will draw you until myself." So, God so loved the world that he gave his son Jesus to show you love by giving up his life. He believes that God has already release his loving angels throughout the earth in this twenty first century.

When you decide to give your heart to Jesus, then the love of God will be deposited into your heart so you can share with others by showing and speaking the love power, this love power will take you on the greatest love journey of your life, through social media.

This is why social media will be her greatest hour on the face of the earth, she will be given the opportunity by God to love and drawn people like it has never been known by social media before. Remember, one day is like a thousand years to the lord, and in Crissa's case, one love hour is like a thousand love hours working through social media.

His point is God can get a lot done in Crissa's one love hour than most who doesn't show love on social media. She has developed as one of the greatest lovers on social media. Her love has become a powerful force and weapon that has been revealed to the social media.

Her mission is to accept the love mission to the world of basketball, to be able to release this love through social media. Remember, she is daddy little girl no matter how big she gets or how old she becomes, he has a commitment to serve her through love for the rest of his life.

He would like to extend to you the opportunity to help him, help her by contacting her on one of her sites. Please listen to his words that is way deep down inside of his heart to love his little girl. He is asking you by the Holy Spirit to begin to show Crissa some love on social media.

You and her together spiritually will see great things happen not only for daddy's little girl but for you too. You see, by you planting seeds into daddy's little girl, your love will help her to rise to stardom one day, you will been using foresight in the year 2021-2025, you will help bring great results in her love life through social media.

This is the sowing and planting principle that steers up the natural and produces a spiritual manifestation of a love harvest as soon as you apply the principles. You have finally reached the sowing, planting, and investing area of the final frontier, not too many people are aware of the concept and principles.

This would be the perfect time in your life to accept this mission and test it to see how good God will be to you. Base on the information that he researched on the internet by "Marketo," the definite guide to social media marketing states that the impact of social media transcends in every aspect of your daily lives.

He is talking about work, politics, breaking news, and he wants you to be able to see and understand how you can be a tool that is able to help daddy's little girl. Today, social media is used universally by consumers and brands companies and is one of the most effective channels to connect you to people.

Social media works with your followers, and this is one of the reasons why he is writing this chapter so you can show daddy's little girl a little love. Social media marketing refers to the process of gaining traffic or attention through their sites.

Social media itself is a catch-all term for sites that may provide radically different social actions. For instance, Twitter is a social site designed to let people share short messages or "updates" with others. Social media marketing offers daddy's little girl and others a vast opportunity to engage with their buyers, across the entire customer lifecycle, on the platforms they actively tune in for information.

As a marketer and supporter, you can help daddy's little girl to build her brand, drive demand, and engage her buyers. Daddy's little girl will be able to manage social media marketing on a day-to-day basis with your help and support.

This will include all her activities about things that she will be able to target her followers and customers, because the love of social media will grow inside of her to build her followers. She will pull from her past and presence experience to further her business opportunity.

In the year 2021-2025, daddy's little girl will be doing great things through the people hearts, one particular thing is falling in love with the whole concept of social media. One day, she will be able to create and manage all of her images, video's, and followers, because of the love she has grown for social media.

Remember she knows how to fall in love with social media, like she did with basketball. One day, one week, one month and one year, just as she did on the track and court. Daddy's little girl will be able to promote herself through the form of internet marketing that involves the promotion of websites by increasing her visibility through paid advertising.

One day, she will be able to build trust in her followers and supporters because of the love she has for social media. She is now trying to communicate to create conversations everyday through the networks of social media in love.

If you know anyone who is technically sound with the latest technology of social media, please show some love Crissa way. Daddy's little girl will try to keep her followers engaged personally by informing them of every positive move she makes towards success, because true love leaves no one behind.

She will open up her heart of love to all of her consumers to build trust and confidence. She has already learned in the past to accept her mistakes and the mistakes of others and to apologize for her wrongs doings and also love and respect those who are less fortunate.

She is now able to forgive and move forward with all of her followers and consumers, because that is what true love does from the heart. The most promising thing that you have to learn, if not already learned by reading this book, is to share with others what you have found written in the love pages of daddy little girl.

These are the things that you must learn from her experience, to love with compassion, feelings, and emotions for your little girl. Daddy would like for you to confirm in your spirit with God if it would be okay for you to pray for her followers and consumers.

You must believe that the love of God will draw her followers and consumers to a place of hope, belief, endurance, and support as a true follower of Crissa Jackson into "the final frontier of social media. Please allow the warrior inside of you go to battle everyday like she does for her followers.

CHAPTER SEVENTEEN

LOVE
THE FINAL CHAPTER

He has shared a lot of information throughout this book concerning himself and his little girl and he hopes you have taken all the information in to help you and your child to reach the unreachable, to touch the untouchable, to see the unbelievable and hear the un-hearable.

He wants you to know that this book was impregnate inside of him with God's love, he believes you will become impregnate so you are able to give birth spiritually from what you learn about this true love story that is able to help you on your love journey.

In other words, this book is about sharing the love of God, so you would get the opportunity to get this true love message and apply it to all of your love ones that are playing sports. This will give you the opportunity to be successful on your journey and adventure pursuing the love of sports.

Please, do not get the love of God twisted concerning all the false, fake, imitation loves that makes a person wander all over the world of sports for a quick fix. This is a fact, especially when it comes to your personal relationship with your daughter or son.

It is very important that you understand how you and your little girl/boy are going to overcome the obstacles, distractions, and any kind of negatives that will purposely attach themselves to your sport journey.

What he meant earlier by you being twisted concerning God's love is, you can't fake, imitate God's love, God's love is not what appeals to the eyes, ears or some may say, to the lust of the flesh. God's love appeals to the inner part of your heart, it will connect to your mind and mouth while you are on your sports journey.

This is a fact, it's going to take true and real love in order to get the job done, and the only love you should know that can perform in you is the love of God. He wants all the daddies and their little girls and boys to be in the best possible position to overcome day by day, week by week, month by month, and year by year.

The very good thing about this book, it will reveal to you what and how to do everything in love. This is the truth and underlining message, he knew that he was instructed by the Holy Spirit to share this true love story about his little girl and how God commissioned him to write about her story.

God commissioned him to write, so he could share the love to all daddies and their little girls that would benefit from the information. He knew, the love process would draw all daddies and theirs little girls to God's love for success in sports.

This was an appointed time in his life to write about a true love story, he felt in his spirit would give birth into the minds and hearts of so many people that are searching for true love. This was a one-shot opportunity for him and he believes he nail it in Jesus name.

He knew that this true love story would open the window of heaven to reveal the true love of God. He knew spiritually, it would give everyone the opportunity to be able to get meaning and understanding about the true love of game of your choice.

His purpose is to inspired anyone who dares to start on the love road to their love journey, seeking the love of the game of basketball or the sport of their choice. Love will be the common denominator for the both of them through practicing and training.

God's love was designed to perform things like dedication, loyalty, commitment, faithfulness and joyfulness to whatever sport you set out to train and practice. It will not be hard for the both of you to discover that the love of God will become the open and final chapter in both of your lives.

How you will know if love is the open and final chapter, love will be in whatever you do or say when it comes to the sport of your choice. God's love will become the center of your known world of sports and will give you hope, faith, and endurance in every area of the sport of your choice.

The final chapter also means, you have reached the end of the book and now you are ready for the love journey of sports. He also would like to close this chapter with a prayer to God for all you daddies/mommies and little girls/boys.

It is important to him that all daddies or mommies and little girls or boys, who are going to come together to start or continue on one of the greatest journey of all times, concerning the love of the game of sports, you must read every chapter in this book.

He prays that the Holy Spirit of God will give you both a spiritual touch of love to draw you together like never before in the history of your known days and give you both the victories to all of your conquests. He also asks God, to deposit his love in the both of you, to fall in love with each other over and over again.

He is also asking God, to help you guys to pray and fast, to trust the process of love for both to believe all things, hope in all things,

and endure all things and know that love will never fail you while you are on the love journey of sports.

He also gives thanks and praise to God for his glory for all the reading you have done in this book. He worships God for his love, he has shared with you about the love of the game. He asks, all daddies and mommies to have faith through love that your little girl and boy can become love fires for the game of sports.

Amen

About the Author

He is a father who is in love with all of his kids unto death do they part, a person who is in love with God, and a father who gave his best love offering to his daughter at the age of six years old by training her for twelve years, 364 days a year give or take.

He is a man who has grown to love according to the word of God and to love with all of his heart, mind, body, strength, and soul. A man who has learned that faith works through God's love and that love is the answer to all things.

He is a love messenger for Jesus Christ, an evangelist to the lost souls, an author who understands that the spiritual church needs God's love in order to reach the unreachable. He is a person who wants to send a message to the world about love, he knows that this generation is the love dispensation of 2020-2025.

He knows where sin abounds, God's grace (love & mercy) will abound even stronger. He understands being a messenger of love is his duty to serve you in the spirit of love, so you would be able to discern the truth of the mystery and the unknown of the spirit of true love.

He also wanted you to be fully aware of the knowledge of love principles and concepts concerning true love. This is who he is, this is who he became and this is him, "*The Love Messenger.*" This book is about a little girl who started training for basketball at the age of six years old and has not stop, and she is now in her thirties give or take.

This book is also dedicated to his daughter, Aleena Jackson, who went on to be with Jesus (September 21, 2020). This book is part of "Liberty Evangelistic Ministry," all monies that is made from this book, will go into the ministry bank account, to be disperse by the author as he is led by the spirit of true love.